Resilient SCHOOL LEADERS

STRATEGIES FOR TURNING ADVERSITY INTO ACHIEVEMENT

JERRY L. PATTERSON

PAUL KELLEHER

ASSOCIATION FOR SUPERVISION AND CURRICULUM DEVELOPMENT
ALEXANDRIA, VIRGINIA USA

Association for Supervision and Curriculum Development
1703 N. Beauregard St. • Alexandria, VA 22311-1714 USA
Phone: 800-933-2723 or 703-578-9600 • Fax: 703-575-5400
Web site: http://www.ascd.org • E-mail: member@ascd.org
Author guidelines: http://www.ascd.org/write

Gene R. Carter, *Executive Director;* Nancy Modrak, *Director of Publishing;* Julie Houtz, *Director of Book Editing & Production;* Deborah Siegel, *Project Manager;* Georgia Park, *Senior Graphic Designer;* Circle Graphics, *Typesetter;* Vivian Coss, *Production Specialist*

All Web links in this book are correct as of the publication date below but may have become inactive or otherwise modified since that time. If you notice a deactivated or changed link, please e-mail books@ascd.org with the words "Link Update" in the subject line. In your message, please specify the Web link, the book title, and the page number on which the link appears.

Paperback ISBN: 1-4166-0267-4 • ASCD product #104003   s11/05
e-books: retail PDF ISBN: 1-4166-0368-9 • netLibrary ISBN: 1-4166-0366-2 • ebrary ISBN: 1-4166-0367-0

Quantity discounts for the paperback book: 10–49 copies, 10%; 50+ copies, 15%; for 500 or more copies, call 800-933-2723, ext. 5634, or 703-575-5634.

Library of Congress Cataloging-in-Publication Data

Patterson, Jerry L., 1944-
  Resilient school leaders : strategies for turning adversity into achievement / Jerry L. Patterson and Paul Kelleher.
      p. cm.
  Includes bibliographical references and index.
  ISBN 1-4166-0267-4 (alk. paper)
  1. School management and organization. 2. Educational leadership. I. Kelleher, Paul, 1943- II. Title.
  LB2805.P33184 2005
  371.2—dc22
                                                                    2005023983

12 11 10 09 08 07 06 05   12 11 10 9 8 7 6 5 4 3 2 1

Resilient
SCHOOL LEADERS

STRATEGIES FOR TURNING ADVERSITY INTO ACHIEVEMENT

INTRODUCTION

This book strives to respond to the basic question "How can leaders move ahead in the face of adversity?" We define *leaders* broadly to include those who occupy positions of formal authority and those who informally lead others because of their expertise, credibility, and relationships. The book is written for leaders who have faced adversity in the past, wrestle with adversity right now, or anticipate adversity in the future. Chances are, this book is written for you. Its foundation rests on our firm belief, substantiated throughout the book by current research and best practices, that you can move ahead despite the storms in your life. Our focus is on you as leader, storms in your life, and strategies to help you navigate the storms to safe harbor.

Metaphor of Storms

The typical image of adversity seems to be almost exclusively a negative one. We have found from our own experience that many leaders don't want to acknowledge adversity in their lives because they believe it conveys a sign of weakness in leadership. For example, soon after the book *Bouncing Back* (Patterson, Patterson, & Collins, 2002) was published, some criticized its title. As one superintendent confessed, "I was reluctant to have people seeing me reading a book about bouncing back. Bouncing back means that I have been knocked to the ground. Good superintendents don't acknowledge they have been sucker-punched by adversity, knocked down, and then scrambled to bounce back." We think the metaphor of storms aptly captures the spirit behind the word *adversity*. Just as storms in nature always end and the sun always comes out again, adversity in our lives always ebbs, and we can emerge stronger from it.

Storms symbolically represent significant and unplanned disruptions to expectations for how life will unfold. Storms can range from the warm, soft rain of a spring day to the wind-driven, needle-sharp sleet of a winter gale. Storms can be as relatively innocuous as a weak, low-pressure area passing through with clouds and drizzle or as strong and dangerous as a hurricane or tornado. Contexts—such as season and geography—can make all the difference with storms. The moisture of a soaking rain in spring in the south can produce a life-threatening blizzard or ice storm in winter in the north. Similar storms can produce different outcomes.

The storms of school life are also exceedingly varied in kind and intensity. They can range from the inconvenience and frustration caused when inclement weather cancels outdoor activity at an elementary school, to angry public controversies over grading policies, to the devastating disruption caused when a student dies. The varied contexts of school storms will also produce different outcomes. A school with a stable, respected leader and a trusted faculty will weather a public controversy much more successfully than a school that has a history of an adversarial relationship with its community.

Storms of nature and storms of school life share predictable unpredictability. Although we know that storms inevitably will occur, we don't know, even with the best forecasts, exactly when they will hit or with what intensity. And we cannot be sure what the contextual factors will be—the temperature, the wind conditions, or the school climate—when the storms strike. Your challenge as school leader is to weather the storm and apply your skills to strengthen your resilience after the storm has subsided.

Research Base for the Book

We drew from a diverse research base in preparing to write this book, looking outside the field of education to the disciplines of individual psychology, sociology of organizations, and organizational development, as well as philosophy and the wisdom of experience. One source of practical experience included our own careers in education, collectively serving more than 70 years in a variety of roles that include teacher, principal, central office administrator, superintendent, and university teacher.

Another primary source of practical wisdom and experience were educational leaders like you. We identified 25 people who represent reflective writers in the area of leadership as well as reflective practitioners who are educational leaders in the field. Listed here are the leaders we interviewed (see the appendix for more extensive biographies):

Roland Barth	Peter Block	Ben Canada
Gene Carter	Carol Choye	Loucrecia Collins
Vince Ferrandino	Charles Fowler	Michael Fullan
Herman Gaither	Maria Goodloe	Linda Hanson
Paul Houston	Larry Lezotte	Jim Loehr
Josephine Moffett	Rubén Olivárez	Gerrita Postlewait
Phillip Schlechty	Chuck Schwahn	Tom Sergiovanni
Lynne Shain	Dennis Sparks	Alicia Thomas
Dan Wertz		

We are indebted to these individuals, who graciously extended the time, reflection, and insights to make the interviews special. With more than 700 years of collective experience, their perspectives enriched our research base, and their comments are included extensively throughout the book.

This book is a journey toward resilience in the face of life's storms. It is founded on principles of optimism, hope, and efficacy. We believe in optimism—your ability to maintain a positive outlook about the future, despite the adversities that inevitably will occur. We believe in hope—your passion to fight through the storms for what is right, just, and reasonable, irrespective of the outcomes. We believe in the power of efficacy—your confidence in your own capabilities. Our hope for this book is that you will gain keen insights, proven strategies, and a heightened sense of efficacy to help you navigate the storms and emerge from them stronger than before.

1

A Deeper Meaning
of Resilience

Resilience is a convenient label to describe things that bounce back. Newspaper headlines declared the winners of the 2004 World Series, the Boston Red Sox, a "resilient" team. A manufacturer chose "Resilience" as the brand name for its pantyhose. The trait of resilience has, in fact, been used to describe a range of human performance, from Lance Armstrong's battle with cancer to New York City's courage following 9/11. But resilience is more than a trendy topic. Resilience is a multidimensional, research-based construct that offers a powerful set of tools to help school leaders grow stronger from adversity. Our intent in this book is to take you on a journey to strengthen your understanding and leadership skills in the area of resilience.

A Brief History of Resilience

Resilience finds its home in the field of psychology. For many years, the psychologists' view was a negative one. Shortly after World War II, the National Institutes of Health began to fund large grants to research psychologists, provided that their line of inquiry was mental disorders. "Psychologists became dedicated chroniclers of mental illness, exploring the many varieties and developing convoluted categories and subcategories of disorders with increasing zeal" (Reivich & Shatte, 2002, p. 57).

The problem-focused medical model spilled over into other domains of psychology. Researchers described resilience in terms of the coping factors needed to survive an array of risk factors, including family dysfunction, disease, illness, and chronic poverty. Researchers employed a deficits model, studying how people narrowed the gap between their deficits due to adversity and what they needed to function in survival mode.

A breakthrough in thinking occurred in 1998 when the president of the American Psychological Association, Martin Seligman, called for movement away from the deficits model to a strengths model typically described as *positive psychology*. Positive psychology has two basic goals: (1) to increase understanding of human strengths through the development of classification systems and methods to measure the strengths and (2) to infuse this knowledge into effective programs and interventions designed to build participants' strengths rather than repair their weaknesses (Reivich & Shatte, 2002, p. 58). Positive psychology emphasizes three points: *positive experiences* such as happiness, pleasure, joy, and fulfillment; *positive individual traits* such as character, talents, and strengths; and *positive institutions* such as families, schools, businesses, communities, and societies (Pearsall, 2003, p. 7).

A parallel shift in psychological research caught the public's attention when Werner and Smith (1992) published *Overcoming the Odds: High Risk Children from Birth to Adulthood*. For more than 30 years, the researchers followed into adulthood the lives of 505 children born on the island of Kauai in Hawaii. Werner and Smith found that about one-third of the boys and girls in this cohort were considered high-risk children because they had been born into poverty and had experienced moderate to severe degrees of perinatal stress, or because they lived in a family environment troubled by discord, divorce, parental alcoholism, or mental illness (Werner & Smith, 1992, p. 192). So far, this scenario sounds more like the deficits model of psychology. But the researchers report that within this subset of high-risk children, about one out of three grew into a competent young adult who, according to the researchers, "loved well, worked well, played well, and expected well. None developed serious learning or behavioral problems in childhood or adolescence" (p. 192). Moreover, these high-risk children succeeded in school and in their personal lives, and they expressed a strong desire to take advantage of whatever opportunities were available after high school. The conclusions from Werner and Smith's study offer a hopeful perspective for those beset by adversity. People faced with chronic or crisis adversity can rise above the survival mode, transition through the recovery mode, and find the necessary strength to grow into resilience.

A substantial number of strength-oriented studies followed on the heels of Werner and Smith's work, and today researchers continue to add empirical evidence supporting the premise that resilience is not a fixed-trait phenomenon. Resilience is developmental, it can be learned, and it can be taught. The research findings reported in this book show that leaders can apply this developmental model in their own professional and personal lives. Using a strengths emphasis, we show school leaders how to draw upon their personal assets to move ahead in the face of adversity.

Three Dimensions of Resilience

We define *resilience* as using your energy productively to emerge from adversity stronger than ever. But, as noted at the beginning of the chapter, resilience has more depth than a one-sentence description suggests. Three dimensions form a comprehensive resilience framework: the *interpretation* of current adversity and future possibility, the *resilience capacity* to tackle adversity, and the *actions* needed to become more resilient in the face of the adversity (see Figure 1.1). In subsequent chapters, we develop each of these dimensions in detail.

Dimension of Interpretation

Something bad happens. You react. Something happens because of your reaction. You react again. This cause-and-effect chain reaction depicts a stimulus-response theory, $S \rightarrow R$, that early psychologists used to explain the course of events following adversity. Current theory, along with supporting research, adds the variable of *interpretation* into the equation $S \rightarrow I \rightarrow R$. Adversity, the stimulus (S), unexpectedly occurs in your life. You interpret (I) the adversity, drawing on your sense of what led to the adversity, what or who actually caused the adversity, what risks are posed because of the adversity, and what the future holds as a result of the adversity. Based on your interpretation of these variables, you choose to respond (R).

Applying this equation to the construct of resilience, you choose how you interpret bad things that happen to you. Imagine that the interpretation dimension shown in Figure 1.1 serves as a master filter that all stimuli must pass through before a response is selected. This filter is perhaps the single most powerful factor in predicting your resilience level in the aftermath of the storm. How you choose to interpret things that happen to you shapes your overall outlook, whether it is your general

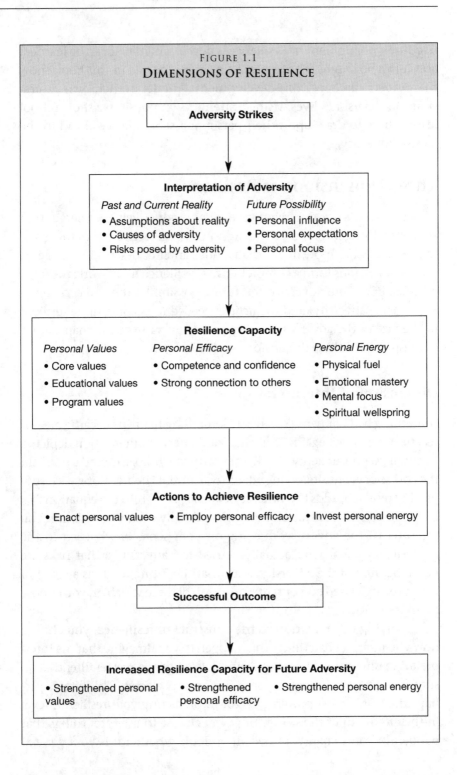

FIGURE 1.1
DIMENSIONS OF RESILIENCE

Adversity Strikes

Interpretation of Adversity

Past and Current Reality
- Assumptions about reality
- Causes of adversity
- Risks posed by adversity

Future Possibility
- Personal influence
- Personal expectations
- Personal focus

Resilience Capacity

Personal Values
- Core values
- Educational values
- Program values

Personal Efficacy
- Competence and confidence
- Strong connection to others

Personal Energy
- Physical fuel
- Emotional mastery
- Mental focus
- Spiritual wellspring

Actions to Achieve Resilience
- Enact personal values
- Employ personal efficacy
- Invest personal energy

Successful Outcome

Increased Resilience Capacity for Future Adversity
- Strengthened personal values
- Strengthened personal efficacy
- Strengthened personal energy

outlook on life or your outlook specifically connected to adversity that enters your life. So, in effect, your interpretation is an expression of your level of *relative* optimism (or pessimism) about life.

Operationally, we define relative optimism along a four-point scale: unrealistic pessimism, realistic pessimism, realistic optimism, and unrealistic optimism. Chapter 2 develops these concepts in detail; for now we present the following definitions:

• *Unrealistic pessimists* have a pervasive, rather permanent negative interpretation of adversity that happens to them, and they have no confidence that anything positive will come out of the adversity.

• *Realistic pessimists* have a reasonably accurate interpretation of reality, but they hold a bleak view of the future and don't think their effort will make much of a difference.

• *Realistic optimists* seek to understand fully what is really going on, including how they may have played a role in causing the adversity. They also believe that they can make a difference in the future despite the constraints imposed by reality.

• *Unrealistic optimists* are quick to make judgments about reality without taking the necessary time to digest what is truly happening. They underestimate the risks that adversity poses, and they firmly believe that they can make their highest hopes become reality in the face of storms they encounter.

As a school leader, many times you don't have a choice about the nature and intensity of adversity you confront. But you do have a choice in how you interpret the adversity. In Chapter 3, we draw from our interviews with educational leaders to demonstrate how you can apply the skills of the realistic optimist to bolster your resilience.

Dimension of Resilience Capacity

Adversity can be chronic or crisis generated. School leaders who function in an environment characterized by high poverty, high student mobility, and low community support know all about chronic adversity. In *No Excuses: Lessons from 21 High-Performing, High-Poverty Schools*, Carter (2001) addresses the chronic adversity faced by schools of the United States' poorest children. He cites these statistics: "Fifty-eight percent of low-income 4th graders cannot read, and 61 percent of low-income 8th graders cannot do basic math. Of the roughly 20 million low-income children in K–12 schools, 12 million aren't even learning the most elementary skills" (p. 1). One can debate the details, but Carter's major point engenders little argument: A significant percentage of the nation's schoolchildren struggle with chronic adversity, and the impact of this adversity is felt in schools each day. As Carter amplifies in his book, despite chronic adversity, there are many rich examples of school leaders and teachers who work daily with resilient students to produce high performance in the classrooms.

Crisis-generated adversity usually produces a more immediate shock and challenge to a leader's resilience because it hits with incredible force and intensity. Death and violence are two extreme cases of crisis adversity. Less dramatic crises, such as serious budget shortfalls and community or district scandals, can lead to major disruptions to normal conditions. Even though no one wishes for crises, a crisis can in fact serve as a catalyst to resilience. According to Sull and Houlder (2005), crises sometimes force you to make choices. The loss of a job or an unexpected denial of promotion, for example, can be the catalyst for exploring what you really want to make of your working life. Crises can also force you to reexamine your commitments. Sudden news of an aging parent's serious illness can cause you to put your work pressures in perspective, redistributing your time and energy in ways that are most important to you.

Large or small, chronic or crisis, adversity happens. How you respond is determined in part by your resilience capacity when tough times strike. Let's assume that the resilience capacity frame in Figure 1.1 visually depicts your resilience tank. The amount of fuel in this tank is the raw material you have to draw on to propel you through the storm to safe ground. Three fuel sources make up your resilience capacity: personal values, personal efficacy, and personal energy.

At any given time, the boundaries of your resilience capacity are determined by life's accumulated experiences. The good news is that resilience capacity is elastic over time. As you grow from adversity, you expand your resilience capacity through strengthened personal values, efficacy, and energy. This expanded capacity provides more fuel for you to face the future. Of course, the opposite can happen if you react to adversity negatively. You remain stuck in the victim role, draining your resilience capacity. Our emphasis, consistent with the resilience research cited earlier in the field of positive psychology, is on a strengths perspective, not a weakness perspective. We don't place judgment (nor should you) on your current resilience capacity. Today's capacity is today's reality. Granted, your capacity may be *relatively* smaller than you would prefer. But we demonstrate throughout the book that you can do something about it. For now, we provide an overview of the three sources of resilience capacity.

Personal Values. Personal values consist of three tiers of values that represent a personal values hierarchy. At the top of the hierarchy are the deeply held *core values* that define what you stand for as an individual. They transcend time and context. Core values include ethical principles about what is right and wrong, such as trust, fairness, and citizenship. Core values also entail individualized values that define what matters most to you. Examples of individualized core values are compassion and a balanced life.

Resting just below the core values level in the hierarchy are your *primary educational values*. These are values about what matters most to you in your role as school leader. Do you value the importance of all students achieving at proficient levels? Do you value a culture of open communication?

The third category in the personal values hierarchy is your belief in the area of *program values,* the values that guide your actions related to specific program initiatives in your organization. For example, what do you value in areas such as middle school language arts instruction, high school assessment systems, or parental involvement?

Your personal value system, previewed here and developed fully in Chapters 4 and 5, is a significant part of the currency you have in your resilience bank account.

Personal Efficacy. Another important source of resilience capacity is personal efficacy, or your belief in your capacity to accomplish challenging goals. Personal efficacy is composed of two key building blocks: your sense of self-confidence and competence and your strong connections to others who support your efforts.

Simply put, confidence and competence mean "*I am capable.* I have the skills, the knowledge, and the attitudes to tackle whatever is thrown at me." To illustrate how this concept applies to your own professional life, imagine the following scenario:

> You arrive at school on a Monday morning and discover the local
> TV news van in the school parking lot. As you approach your

designated parking space, a veteran teacher rushes to meet you with the news that two students were struck by a car driven by the school secretary. Not far behind the teacher is a swarm of TV cameras with a parade of emergency vehicles roaring in the background. Adversity has struck. Your resilience capacity to move through this tragedy is shaped significantly by how capable you feel to handle the crisis. You respond by reminding yourself, "I have handled other school tragedies, and we emerged in strong fashion. I have confidence that I can provide the leadership skills necessary for us to get through this one, too."

As this example illustrates, confidence and competence are inextricably linked. Past competence ("I have handled other school tragedies") directly affects present confidence ("I can get through this one, too"), which in turn affects present competence and future confidence, leading to a positive upward spiral of improved performance. Strong self-confidence and competence combine to create the belief that you can make a difference.

The reciprocal influences of confidence and competence can, unfortunately, also create a negative spiral that leads to diminished performance. Some leaders hold the mind-set, "I may have the skills to get through this stuff, but it won't make a difference anyway. So why bother?" Such a belief system isn't strong enough to get you through the tough times to a better place in the future. Lower self-confidence and a weaker sense of competence lead to less effective performance.

If you have a strong sense of personal efficacy, you believe in yourself, and you believe that you can influence the outcomes of adverse circumstances hurled at you. You demonstrate *"I can make a difference. I have the competence, the leadership skills, to get us through this tragedy, and I have the confidence that I can make a difference in helping us emerge from this stronger than ever as a school community."*

In the midst of tough times, just believing in yourself isn't necessarily enough to get you through adversity in a healthy way. You need another building block to lean heavily on: *"I have the resources available to support me."* Returning to the prior scenario, your resilience capacity is influenced by your realization that you alone can't successfully lead the organization through the crisis. You need to call on the skills and experience of the school social worker, the crisis management team, and the agency contracted to help with death and dying issues in the school district. Prior to taking any action, you may also decide to call a peer, a mentor, a friend, or an intimate partner to seek advice or to talk through a proposed plan of action.

Reaching out for support is not a sign of a personal weakness that you can't take care of things by yourself. Believing that you have resources to draw upon is a sign of strength. So when trouble comes, you increase your chance of successfully leading others through the storm by seeking help and support in meeting whatever challenge is thrown your way.

Personal Energy. Personal energy is another vital component of your resilience tank. *Energy,* a physics principle, is defined as the capacity to do work. So your resilience energy is a latent resource that you draw upon when you are ready to do the work needed to move ahead in the face of adversity. Energy comes in four types: physical, emotional, mental, and spiritual.

According to Jim Loehr, a leading researcher and trainer of athletes to achieve high performance, physical fuel is a crucial energy source.

> Physical energy is the *fundamental* source of fuel, even if our work is almost completely sedentary. It not only lies at the heart of alertness and vitality but also affects our ability to manage our emotions, sustain concentration, think creatively, and even maintain our commitment to whatever mission we are on. Leaders and managers make a fundamental mistake when they assume that they can overlook the physical dimension of energy and still expect those who work for them to perform at their best. (Loehr & Schwartz, 2003, p. 48)

Physical energy is measured in terms of quantity, and it is available to you, in the strictest sense, 24 hours a day. During emergency conditions, workers such as firefighters and rescue units are expected to perform 24 hours or more at a time without significant breaks. Until recent legislation intervened, medical doctors serving as residents also routinely worked more than 100 hours in a given week. Now, medical residents are required by law to limit their physical energy output to 80 hours a week. Many school leaders report comparable energy expense, especially when crisis erupts.

Positive emotions increase energy and enthusiasm to take on challenges. Negative emotions sap energy and willingness to work. Emotional mastery, then, is your capacity to manage emotions skillfully in order to maximize positive feelings that produce positive energy and full engagement in your work and to minimize negative feelings that reduce energy and distract from effective performance.

Mental energy provides the capacity to organize yourself and focus your attention under stress. When you are hit with adversity, the circumstances usually call for more physical energy and generate more emotional energy. With these demands, it becomes an even greater challenge to channel your mental energy by staying focused and mentally acute.

Spiritual energy is the fourth ingredient comprising your personal energy. Loehr and Schwartz (2003) underscore the power of spiritual energy in affecting your resilience capacity:

> Fundamentally, spiritual energy is a unique source for action in all our lives. It is the most powerful source for our motivation, perseverance, and direction. We define spiritual not in the religious sense, but rather in more simple and elemental terms: the connection to a deeply held set of values and to a purpose beyond our self-interest. At the practical level, anything that ignites the human spirit serves to drive full engagement and to maximize performance in whatever mission we are on. (p. 110)

Your wellspring of spiritual energy anchors you in a set of universal principles about humanity. It reflects your capacity to overcome adversity in support of a cause that is beyond your own self-interest.

In summary, your resilience capacity to tackle adversity depends on the personal values you hold, the personal efficacy you possess, and the personal energy you have available. At any point in time, these three areas define your capacity to move ahead. We take a more in-depth look at each category in later chapters.

Dimension of Action

You move from capacity to strength when you add the resilience dimension of action. You act on your values, act consistent with your commitment to make a difference, and act by drawing on the reservoir of energy stored in your resilience tank. In Chapters 4 and 5, we use examples from our interviews to illustrate how you can more clearly convey your values and align them with your actions to strengthen resilience in the face of a storm. For now we reiterate that resilience strength is the sum of the dynamic interaction among three dimensions of resilience: interpretation, capacity, and action. The following story shared during our interview with Larry Lezotte, a consultant and preeminent spokesperson for continuous school improvement, captures these dynamics.

Lezotte was 5 years old when he contracted polio. This was during the late 1940s, when polio struck in epidemic proportions. As he described the sequence of events in his struggle with polio, he first talked about how his family responded to the *interpretation* dimension. Regarding the reality of the current situation, he said, "My condition got progressively worse until it got to the point where they had an iron lung outside my room, ready to put me in it. A lot of people back then went into iron lungs and were there for life." Lezotte said his parents refused to interpret the future bleakly. "My family and I had high expectations and hope so deep that we refused to give up. It was a powerful factor in how we responded to my condition."

The family's dimension of *resilience capacity* was boosted by a strong set of values, a sense of efficacy that "we can work on this and make a difference in Lezotte's life." In addition, his parents called upon their strong Catholic faith. In Lezotte's words, "My parents prayed to God to tell them what to do. The thing that came out of it was that I needed to be taken to Ann Arbor, Michigan, for medical consultation."

Lezotte's parents made the trip. As they were leaving the hospital in Ann Arbor, a nurse quietly approached them, saying, "Let me tell you about a certain treatment where they take wool rags, put them in very hot water, and then wrap the affected legs. I want you to meet me out in the back parking lot. I am going to steal a set of these materials, and I want you to take them home and use them." Lezotte's parents did as they were told.

The resilience dimension of *action* involved his parents' following through with the nurse's instructions. "My dad and mother worked night and day with the materials, and in between they worked every joint of my body. In three months they had me up and walking. In the 8th grade, I got scoliosis and had to have nine vertebrae fused, which led to my spending almost a year in bed."

But Lezotte and his family could not be deterred. Their continued actions produced small gains, and, over time, Lezotte's resilience became stronger. He refused to give up. He even played hockey in high school.

Today he plays golf. Out of caring and concern, people have suggested that Lezotte get a medical letter so he can have a disabled parking sticker. Lezotte's response to them reflects his resilience: "I don't need to. There is always going to be a spot that is close enough that I can walk."

Larry Lezotte does not consider himself a hero or a special role model. He is, however, an optimist who demonstrates how a person can apply the dimensions of interpretation, resilience capacity, and action to emerge from adversity stronger than ever.

The Resilience Cycle

Larry Lezotte's adversity eventually made him stronger. But the rebound did not occur overnight. Even the most resilient individuals experience a roller coaster effect as they work through storms. We have identified four phases in a resilience cycle that you as school leader move through when adversity enters your life (Figure 1.2):

1. Deteriorating
2. Adapting
3. Recovering
4. Growing

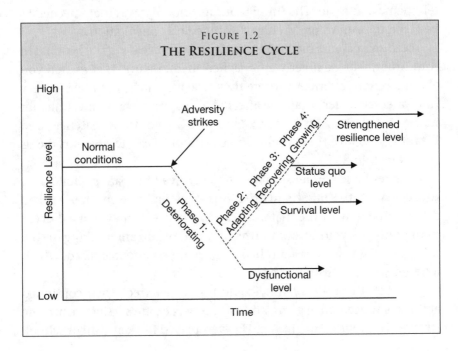

FIGURE 1.2
THE RESILIENCE CYCLE

The cycle, illustrated in Figure 1.2, begins after a disruption to what we're calling *normal conditions*. We realize that some school leaders would take issue with our contention that today's school environment contains any hint of normalcy. However, we also recognize that most leaders would not characterize their jobs as filled with constant, relentless adversity. In the rare situation where a school leader's daily life actually is filled with ongoing adversity, this quality often becomes a new definition of normal for the leader. We make the assumption, then, that the resilience cycle you experience begins with so-called normal conditions. Fortunately, some individuals maintain their resilience primarily in the normal conditions mode. One person we interviewed said, "During my whole life, I really haven't had many setbacks. I had one traumatic incident with the school board, but other than that I can't think of anything. I have been the one in control of my agenda."

Most people aren't so fortunate. Another interviewee began the conversation this way: "In anticipation of this interview, I gave some thought to adversity that I have gone through recently. About eight years ago, my 23-year-old nephew was murdered. He had come out of an apartment, and some guys murdered him kind of as a lark. About a year ago my granddaughter, who was 5, was diagnosed with leukemia. And two weeks after she was diagnosed, my youngest daughter was diagnosed with double pulmonary pneumonia, and we didn't know if she was going to live or not. So when I look at my job, there's nothing that even comes close to this kind of adversity."

Your experience with adversity probably falls between the extremes discussed above. Something happens to disrupt what for you are "normal conditions"—that is, your expectations about what is going to occur in significant areas of your life. Adversity strikes. Of course, not every disruption to your expectations may qualify as adversity. If you expect a meeting to be finished by 2:00 p.m. and it drags on until 4:00 p.m., this disruption probably isn't significant to you. However, we want to underscore that the threshold measure of "significance" resides in the eyes of the beholder. A crisis in the life of an elementary principal may be just another event in the eyes of the superintendent. The messy conditions of leading a school district produce more complex issues cooking in the crucible of adversity than the typical principal confronts. But perception is reality. If it seems like adversity to the leader most directly affected by the disruption to expectations, then it passes the litmus test of adversity.

Phase 1: Deteriorating

After adversity hits, virtually everyone encounters the first stage in the resilience cycle: *deteriorating.* Pearsall (2003) describes the deteriorating phase by stating, "We react like kindling wood being added to fire. At least for a while, we think in ways that cause our problems to heat up and become more intense. We become angry and even aggressive. We blame others or degrade ourselves. We become our own and our problems' worst enemy" (pp. 8–9). Denial, grief, and anger thrust you into the victim role for a time. This is an unhealthy phase to be stuck in, but in the short term the downturn from normal can be healthy if you handle your anger and frustration constructively. The good news is that for a vast percentage of people, the deteriorating phase is temporary. Rarely do individuals plateau out of the deteriorating phase into the dysfunctional level indicated in Figure 1.2. School leaders who find themselves stuck long-term at the dysfunctional level likely will not be able to continue functioning in their professional position.

Phase 2: Adapting

After experiencing the downward-sloping deteriorating phase, most school leaders bounce back to reverse the trajectory upward to the *adapting phase* when they take personal actions to turn things around. Gerrita Postlewait, the superintendent of the Horry County, South Carolina, school district, said, "One swift kick overnight is about all I need, and then I get up and double my efforts. I don't know anything else to do except get back out there and put one foot in front of the other." You adapt to the adversity by reducing anger, confronting your tendency toward denial, and assuming less of a victim role.

This phase should be seen as a necessary transitional step on the way to someplace better. It is not a healthy place to plateau. Those who do level off here end up trapped in the survival mode. The survival mode conveys a view of barely getting by in the aftermath of tough times. As one leader described his hope for the future, "I just hope I can hang in there for three more years without getting fired. Then I'm eligible for retirement, and I'm outta here." This leader focused his energy in doing whatever it took to keep his job. If it meant playing political games or ignoring conflict about to erupt, that's what the leader did to achieve his goal of survival. Surviving is a necessary step in the process of recovery, but it shouldn't be the final step.

Phase 3: Recovering

Continuing the upward trajectory, the adapting phase gives way to the *recovering phase,* a path back to the maintenance level called status quo. For some school leaders, the ultimate goal is to return to the level of how things were before the storm. "If we can only get through this budget crisis and get back to normal, things will be just fine." If you plateau at the status quo level, you may continue to function adequately, but you don't give yourself a chance to experience the growth that is possible from lessons adversity has to teach you.

Phase 4: Growing

Learning from the adversity, you can make the transition from the recovering phase to the *growing phase* on your way to a sustained level of strengthened resilience. Pearsall (2003) calls this stage the thriving level. "We thrive when we surpass and transcend our prior level of functioning, regain and even accelerate our upward psychological trajectory, and seem to have mentally and emotionally benefited from our suffering. Because of our crisis, we seem to begin to flourish. Thrivers aren't masochists who seek or somehow endure pain better than others, but they do tend to be rational optimists who learn from it, know when to fight or flow with it, and when to give in and move on" (pp. 17–18).

The Cycle Personified

Roland Barth, a consultant and former public school and university educator for many years, typified Pearsall's description of thrivers when he described several professional and personal storms in his life during our interview. One professional storm occurred in his first job as a principal. He was hired as an elementary principal and promptly began to lead the staff toward a British primary model of education. Things turned foul as parents protested the proposed changes. "Some parents didn't want experimentation," Barth explained. "Other parents wanted to be more in charge of what goes on in the school. An angry mother said to me, 'What right do you have, Dr. Barth, to decide what *my* child needs?' Clearly there was a misfit between my values and theirs. I tried to listen to them, but I was not going to sell out to parents. I pressed ahead with what I thought was best for the children."

The biggest storm occurred when Barth was fired. Immediately he lapsed into the deteriorating phase. "It was tremendous adversity. I had my hopes and dreams violated. I was torn apart." But eventually he started on the upturn into the adapting phase. "I realized that I needed to look out after myself. I also needed some healing, so I decided to see a therapist. This turned out to be a very important decision." Next Barth entered the recovering phase by starting to write a book about his adversity. "Writing about it helped me slow things down, be more analytical, and figure out what really happened. In particular, I became more conscious of my own abundant contributions to the conflagration. It's one thing to deal with adversity of the moment. It's another thing to deal with the fallout from adversity. People can deal with the immediate issue, but then there is scar tissue that influences their whole life. For me, writing was my way of dealing with the scar tissue so that I would know better next time how to handle [adversity]."

The writing and reflection helped Barth get beyond the recovering phase and move toward the growing phase. "After writing the book about my adversity, I felt really good about the profession and good about my experience. I even said to my wife that I might do it again. In fact, for my next two jobs as principal, I entered strong and really together. It was a fantastic experience."

Barth also discussed adversity at a personal level. He sat with a pillow propped behind his lower back. He took his special pillow to our lunch date at a local diner. He probably takes his pillow everywhere. The pillow is a constant, visual reminder of chronic back pain that Barth has lived with for more than 20 years.

When back pain first stormed into Barth's life, it disrupted his expectations for the future. He saw long-term limitations on what he could do and felt the immediate limitations of living in pain. From so-called normal conditions of a pain-free back, Barth started on the downward slope of the deteriorating phase of the resilience cycle. "I used to hate my back because it didn't deliver for me," he said. "Stuff like this corrodes your spirit. And the back pain caused me to have to alter my lifestyle. This had pejorative meaning to me at first. I couldn't play squash; I couldn't haul wood; I couldn't do gardening. These were all losses."

After a period of wallowing in the victim role, Barth reversed the trajectory. He shifted into the adapting phase when he assumed some responsibility for his condition. Reluctantly, grudgingly, he opted for surgery. "That relieved some of the pain. But I still had problems. I had to give up squash. That was a sad time, and there was a lot of grieving."

But Barth refused to plateau at the survival level of just getting by. He moved into the recovering phase. At the emotional level of recovering, he took a workshop on befriending your anger. "That was a great concept. If you can befriend [anger], you can expect it, respect it, accept it, and not let it destroy you." He also engaged in physical therapy to help with physically recovering. And Barth made other adjustments to return to normal functioning: "I started using my head rather than my back. For example, I hauled firewood with the help of my nephews." In maintenance mode, Barth today is working hard to keep up a normal lifestyle, even if it means turning to others. With a hint of humility, he said, "Now I ask for help. That's hard for me, because I am fairly independent. But I also stopped condemning myself."

In some areas, Barth took charge of shifting to the growing phase of the resilience cycle. He reached out to find new levels of enjoyment that he would not have experienced without the adverse condition of chronic back pain. "I have altered my lifestyle now in ways that are positive. I love to swim. Being in the water—I just love it! I also get a massage now, and it is heaven. These are two lifestyle changes that I wouldn't have engaged in without the back injury. But they are enrichers, enhancers." Barth added with an undercurrent of pride, "I am even starting to say to myself it is OK to indulge myself."

Roland Barth will never be back to "normal conditions" in the sense of a pain-free back. He plied his resilience skills, however, in moving out of the deteriorating phase, through the adapting phase, and into the recovering phase. He even found ways to grow through his pain to new levels of enjoyment, including indulging himself.

We contend throughout this book that the most desirable, long-term target in the face of adversity is the level of strengthened resilience. The three dimensions of resilience examined in this chapter have a direct, profound influence on the way a person navigates the four phases of the resilience cycle. Your *interpretation* of adversity; your *resilience capacity* in the form of personal values, personal efficacy, and personal energy; and your *action* to move ahead position you to move through the phases in a healthy way. Even after struggling to survive in the face of adversity and after calling forth the necessary strengths to get back to normal, you don't have to be content with just achieving status quo. All along the journey to recovery and beyond, you can consistently, persistently, even relentlessly stay focused on the question "How can I invest my energy productively to emerge from this setback stronger than ever?"

2

OPTIMISM IN THE
FACE OF THE STORM

School leaders remember the good old days when resources were adequate, school boards were stable, superintendents stayed a while, and forces outside the school district trusted those inside the school district to do the best job possible in educating students. It used to be such smooth sailing!

Whether this version of history is fact, illusion, or delusion hardly matters. That was then and this is now. Today few school leaders would characterize their jobs as smooth sailing. In fact, a more apt nautical metaphor is trying to ride out the relentless storms that come and go and come again. In the face of these storms, though, many school leaders construct ways to remain optimistic and move ahead, while some of their colleagues struggle just to tread water, and others eventually drown from the storm. What accounts for such differences?

In our research on resilience in school leaders, we found the answer was best summarized by a well-worn bumper sticker on an old truck: "It's not so much what you do. It's how you think about what you do that makes all of the difference." Your level of optimism, how you interpret the reality of the storm and your future afterward, strongly predicts your ability to come through the storm in a better place. In this chapter, we first examine the meaning and significance of optimism. Next we show how your level of optimism (or pessimism) serves as a filter for interpreting adversity that strikes. We end the chapter with concrete examples showing how your interpretation of adversity directly affects your response to the adversity and your overall resilience.

The Meaning and Significance of Optimism

The scholarly writing on optimism can be traced as far back as Sophocles and Nietzsche, who both argued against optimism, saying it just prolongs human suffering. It is better to face the cold, pessimistic facts of reality and get on with one's life. This negative view of positive thinking lies at the heart of Freud's writings on the topic (Peterson, 2000, p. 45). A shift in position occurred when Taylor and Brown (1988) described a range of studies showing that, generally, people are biased toward optimism as a positive trait. These studies examined constructs such as dispositional optimism (Scheier & Carver, 1992), explanatory style (Buchanan & Seligman, 1995), and big versus little optimism (Peterson, 2000). The most current research reflects another shift, one that views optimism as a trait possessed by all people to varying degrees (Scheier & Carver, 1992; Buchanan & Seligman, 1995; Snyder, 1994).

But even if we all have optimism, specifically what is it? We build a case for a specific brand of optimism we term *realistic optimism*. We define *realistic optimism* as the ability to maintain a positive outlook in the face of adversity without denying the constraints posed by reality. Keep in mind that optimists take the long view. In the short term, even optimists have negative thoughts and feel like victims at times. As Paul Houston, executive director of the American Association of School Administrators, told us, "If you have a short-term view, it is very hard to be resilient, because in the short term, things are going to happen that aren't good. A long-term view makes it almost impossible not to be resilient, because this, too, shall pass. I will have a lot of other shots at this before it is over."

The emphasis is on how you *generally* see the world. We realize that some people dismiss generalizations because they can point to exceptions that contradict the generalization. Other people use generalizations to draw stereotypes of particular categories of individuals. In our use of generalizations, we do not intend to convey either of the possible interpretations just mentioned. Instead, we present generalizations as broad principles that represent patterns over time. Exceptions do occur, and certain individuals do not fit the pattern described by the generalization. Neither case negates the validity of the generalization. Generalizations help people make sense of how the world *generally* works.

Recent research on optimism demonstrates that optimism can be learned (Seligman, 1991) and strengthened (Reivich & Shatte, 2002). The most important discovery, however, is that optimism makes a difference in people's lives. Some of the findings in optimism research include the following:

• Optimistic individuals have better social relationships as well as higher levels of physical health, academic and athletic performance, recovery from illness and trauma, pain tolerance, self-efficacy, and flexibility in thinking (Cameron, Dutton, & Quinn, 2003, p. 53).

• Optimists see adversity as a challenge, transform problems into opportunities, put in hours to refine schools, persevere in finding solutions to difficult problems, maintain confidence, rebound quickly after setbacks, and persist (Schulman, 1999, p. 32).

• Optimists are easily motivated to work harder, are more satisfied and have higher morale, have high levels of motivational aspiration and set stretch goals, persevere in the face of obstacles and difficulties, analyze personal setbacks as temporary, and tend to feel upbeat and invigorated both physically and emotionally (Luthans, 2002).

Peterson (2000) captures the essence of optimism research when he states, "Research is uniform in showing that optimism, however it is measured, is linked to desirable characteristics: happiness, perseverance, achievement, and health" (p. 47).

Degrees of Optimism

Optimism is not an all-or-nothing proposition. It's not a matter of being in the optimist club or out of the club. In fact, your *relative* degree of optimism depends on how you interpret and respond to a series of six key questions:

Past and current reality
• What *assumptions* do I hold about reality?
• What are the *causes* of the current adversity, including my own contribution?
• What are the *risks* posed by the adversity?

Future possibilities
- What is my ability to *influence* future events?
- What are my *expectations* for success?
- What will be the *focus* of my efforts?

These questions are the interpretation filter that you activate to make sense of past and current reality as well as future possibilities growing out of the present adversity. Adversity happens. You interpret what's happening and what could happen in the future. The meaning that you draw from this interpretation shapes how you *choose* to respond. These choices in turn shape your overall outlook, or your relative optimism. Operationally, we describe relative optimism along a four-point scale as shown in Figure 2.1: unrealistic pessimism, realistic pessimism, realistic optimism, and unrealistic optimism. Recall from Chapter 1 that unrealistic pessimists have a pervasive, rather permanent negative interpretation of what's going on, and they have no confidence that anything good will come out of the adversity. Realistic pessimists have a reasonably accurate interpretation of reality, but they take a dim view of the future and don't think it's worth the effort on their part. Realistic optimists work hard to gather needed data to understand current reality, including how they may have personally contributed to a problem. They also take a positive view of the future, believing that they can make a difference, within the constraints of the future. Unrealistic optimists jump to conclusions about current reality without taking time to assess what's really going on. They underestimate the risks posed by adversity and they assume, without a doubt, that they can make the best-case outcomes happen in the future.

To facilitate an understanding of the pessimism–optimism scale, we show how individuals at each point on the scale might respond to the following scenario.

A school principal receives from the superintendent a response to the proposed annual school budget submitted by the principal three weeks earlier. The superintendent's comments are written in red ink—a lot of red ink. In other words, the school budget has several problems, and the superintendent pulls no punches in making known his displeasure with both the process that the school used and the results. The school principal asked for a 10 percent increase in expenditures at a time when the local economy is experiencing a downward trend. The

FIGURE 2.1
PESSIMISM–OPTIMISM SCALE

Category	Unrealistic Pessimists	Realistic Pessimists	Realistic Optimists	Unrealistic Optimists
Interpretation of reality				
Assumptions about reality	Deny that the assumptions are true	Acknowledge that the assumptions are true, magnify their negative impact, and see them as barriers	Acknowledge that the assumptions are true and refuse to accept them as barriers	Dismiss the assumptions as insignificant to progress
Causes of current reality	Find other people and forces totally at fault	Accept some responsibility, but primary cause is others	Accept responsibility for their contribution to the current reality	Assume that they know the causes, but don't invest the time to assess reality accurately
Risks posed by current reality	Greatly overestimate the risks caused by adversity	Understand the risks and place undue weight on the negative	Accurately assess the risks by striving to have enough data to judge	Discount the risks and refuse to see how they may jeopardize the future
Interpretation of future possibilities				
Ability to influence future	Refuse to see how they can make any difference	Believe that any difference they may possibly make won't be worth the personal effort	Believe strongly that they can positively influence the future, within certain constraints	Assume that they will, without a doubt, have a major influence on the future
Expectations for future success	Can't see any possibility for a positive future	Hold low expectations that anything good will happen	Believe that good things may happen, but it will require a lot of work	Assume that the best-case outcomes will happen
Focus of future efforts	Focus exclusively on worst-case outcomes	Heavily emphasize the negative side of the problem	Acknowledge problems, but choose to emphasize the positive possibilities	Focus only on perfect solutions

superintendent wants to know what went wrong and who is primarily responsible for the school budgeting mess.

Using the six key questions posed earlier, let's consider how a school leader at each point on the pessimism–optimism scale interprets adversity. We want to underscore the fact that your relative optimism is shaped over time and becomes your general outlook. So even though we talk here about a specific adversity, the cumulative pattern of responses to adversity determines your relative optimism.

What Assumptions Do I Hold About Reality?

Before we analyze the responses to this question, we need to amplify what we mean by "assumptions about reality." As you experience hardships, your struggle to make sense of what is happening to you is influenced by your interpretation of certain general principles that you hold about the reality of the human condition or, as Phil Schlechty, founder and CEO of the Schlechty Center for Leadership in School Reform, said in his interview, how the world operates. "To really be a leader, you have to be clear to yourself and others about how the world operates," he said. "If you don't have a clear conception of how the world operates, what drives the world, and you can't communicate that in a persuasive way to others, you are not going to be able to lead in tumultuous times."

These principles about the human condition and how the world works are generalizations that you hold, realizing that any particular principle does not universally apply to all people or organizations at all times. You might hold an assumption, for example, that people are basically good. This interpretation of humanity influences how you interpret negative events in your life. You tend to give people the benefit of the doubt when they cause adversity in your life. You see their motives in a positive light, which in turn affects your optimism for moving through the adversity in a healthy way.

At another level, you hold assumptions about the reality of educational organizations. Examples of assumptions about organizational reality include the following:

- Organizations are characterized by complexity, chaos, paradox, and ambiguity.
- Organizations are wired to protect the status quo.

• Organizations are filled with competing goals, power struggles, and political self-interests.

You also hold assumptions about how you generally view the nature of people who work and learn in your educational environment. Do you believe that all students can learn proficiently? Do you believe that educators are intrinsically motivated to do a good job? These assumptions about reality become central to how you view your leadership role in education and how you respond to crisis or chronic adversity. In their research on resilient schools, Patterson and colleagues (2002) report on one low-socioeconomic, high-performing school that passionately believed in the reality that "all students can perform at high performance levels." In the words of the principal, "There are absolutely no excuses for failing to produce achieving students in this school. None. Zero. Zilch. I mean *no excuses*" (p. 33).

Another principal in the same study expressed these sentiments in a similar way. He consistently reminded the teachers, "As long as I am principal in this school, you can be assured that I will not waiver in my belief and expectation that all people, students and adults, can succeed in this school. More pointedly, I expect you to believe and act on the premise, *I believe in you, you can do it, and I won't give up on you.* I expect this to pervade everything you do in this school. The bottom line is, no excuses. Everyone can succeed" (p. 37).

Sometimes beliefs about reality are expressed as assumptions that help guide your practice. Schlechty's Center for Leadership in School Reform holds five basic assumptions (beliefs about reality) that guide all of its work:

• There is an urgent need for dramatic improvement in the performance of America's public schools.
• The key to improving schools is the quality of the work students are provided.
• Students are volunteers. Their attendance can be commanded, but their attention must be earned.
• The changes required to organize schools around students and student work cannot occur unless school districts and communities have or develop the capabilities needed to support change—capacities that are now too often lacking in even the best-run school districts.

- Leadership and leadership development are key components to the creation of district-level capacity to support building-level reform. (Schlechty Center for Leadership in School Reform, 2005)

These beliefs are organizational beliefs. However, they also reflect and are largely derived from the leader's personal beliefs.

To see how assumptions about organizational reality affect the interpretation of adversity, let's return to the scenario described earlier and find out how each person on the pessimism–optimism scale responds to the assumption "Organizations are characterized by complexity and ambiguity."

Unrealistic pessimists deny that this assumption is a characteristic of most organizations, because they don't want to confront the cognitive dissonance that this assumption would inevitably create. In other words, they prefer not to leave their comfort zone in how they regard organizational life. A school leader who fits the profile of an unrealistic pessimist might react to the assumption this way: "The system does indeed have a lot of ambiguity right now. But it doesn't have to be this way. With a few changes by the superintendent, we could restore order and reduce a bunch of the confusion. We could get back to the way organizations are supposed to work in the first place."

Realistic pessimists acknowledge organizations' tendency toward complexity and ambiguity. They see these forces as serious barriers to moving through the adversity in a healthy way. Realistic pessimists believe that the assumption proves their point that the future looks bleak. Consider how the school leader characterized as a realistic pessimist might react to this assumption: "There is little doubt we are working in a place that is complicated and confusing. Moreover, I don't see any way we are going to turn things around anytime in the foreseeable future." Realistic pessimists see the barriers, but they don't see how to overcome them.

Realistic optimists also agree that the assumption is a real force to be reckoned with. Unlike the pessimists, however, realistic optimists don't get trapped in either-or thinking. As a realistic optimist, a school leader might see reality through this lens: "No doubt about it—most organizations are complex and ambiguous. That comes with the territory of organizational life. I need to figure out how I can work within the reality and still move ahead." Realistic optimists see clearly the hurdles posed by the reality of organizations, and they seek ways to clear the hurdles.

Unrealistic optimists give token credence to the assumption, but they dismiss the assumption as unworthy of serious consideration. The school leader who is an unrealistic optimist might offer this perspective: "Yes, that's the way it is around here. But people are always overreacting to the confusion around here. It won't deter me. I will make the best-case outcomes happen." Unrealistic optimists fail to confront the magnitude of the reality. Then, when reality gets in the way of their achieving their lofty goals, they struggle to hold on to their optimism.

As the bumper sticker reminds us, it's not so much what you do. It's how you *think* about what you do that makes all of the difference. How you interpret the reality of organizational life affects your level of optimism and your ability to be successful in the face of reality.

What Are the Causes of the Current Adversity?

Your response to adversity depends in part on what you see as causes of your current predicament. Unrealistic pessimists see the problem as pervasive and permanent. They also blame themselves for the adversity. A school leader who falls into this category might conclude, "The school budget screw-up is going to affect everything that we do around here. It isn't going to go away, and I am responsible for the screw-up. Things can't get any worse." Unrealistic pessimists shoulder all of the weight of blame, exacerbating their feeling of pessimism.

Realistic pessimists acknowledge that they may have some minor responsibility for the adversity but largely see the problem as caused by others. Faced with the same budget mess, a school leader who is a realistic pessimist might be overheard saying, "This budget predicament is indeed really a mess. But my role in the mess is minimal at best. Other folks need to be held accountable for the screw-up." Finding fault with others is a strategy that realistic pessimists use to escape any responsibility for the problem. In turn, as victim, they remain pessimistic about solving the problem.

Realistic optimists accept responsibility that their personal actions contributed in some way to the adversity, and they seek accurate data to understand as clearly as possible how both they and other causes contributed to the problem. A school leader who is a realistic optimist might respond to the budget problem this way: "I need to know as thoroughly as possible what went wrong in the budget planning. I know I had a role in this, and I need to accept responsibility for my contribution to the problem. I also need to understand the other contributing causes so I can make an informed judgment about what to do next." Realistic optimists acknowledge that they played a role in the problem and also know that they can play a role in the solution.

Unrealistic optimists quickly assume that they know the causes, but they are so future directed that they don't invest the time necessary to assess causes of the adversity accurately. They have a false sense of knowing. A school leader who thinks this way might make these comments about the budget snafu: "The cause of our problems is simple. We have a city council who continues to overspend the budget. We have a superintendent who is not clear on parameters about how schools should prepare their budgets. I've been around long enough to know what works. My original budget proposal still stands." For unrealistic optimists, misdiagnosis of the causes produces a miscalculation of the likelihood of success for their agenda.

What Are the Risks Posed by the Adversity?

Unrealistic pessimists overestimate the risks posed by the adversity, creating a feeling of panic and helplessness that pushes them deeper into the victim status. The unrealistic pessimist school leader might believe, "We don't have a chance to get out of this hole. Our entire school program is at significant risk." The high-risk interpretation by unrealistic pessimists fuels their pessimism even more.

Realistic pessimists have a reasonable handle on the risks involved and they interpret the risks negatively. They place heavy emphasis on the perspective that the threat of this adversity is real and serious. A school leader with this orientation may comment, "The risks posed by the downturn in our economy are foreboding for our school. Because of these bleak conditions, we are in serious financial trouble at this school, and I don't see a way out." Realistic pessimists see the glass half empty, and they place considerable weight on the risk of operating at half capacity.

Realistic optimists work hard to accurately assess the risks posed by the adversity because they are committed to making informed judgments about what to do. They don't deny or dismiss the level of threat. In relation to the school budget problems, the realistic optimist leader might observe, "Let's figure out as thoroughly as possible what we are up against. We need to know the real risks involved. With full knowledge, we will have better data to make good decisions about what to do next about our finances." Realistic optimists don't try to skew the risks to fit their overall orientation to problem solving. In fact, their orientation is to get all the facts about risk, as painful as this process may be in the short run, so they can make good decisions in the long run.

Unrealistic optimists, on the other hand, would rather discount the risks than behaviorally minimize them. One research study found that cigarette smokers who were unrealistic optimists avoided trying to quit by adopting self-serving biases that discounted their personal susceptibility to the risks of smoking (Gibbons, Eggleston, & Benthin, 1997). In addition, Reivich and Shatte (2002, p. 55) report that unrealistic optimists underestimate their risks of health problems, and this "It can't happen to me" attitude led them to forgo preventive actions. Applying this pattern to the school leader who is an unrealistic optimist, we might hear the following comments: "People are blowing the financial crisis out of proportion"; "I refuse to dwell on the risks"; "That's negative thinking." Unrealistic optimists dismiss the risks and become frustrated when the risks overwhelm their dreams.

What Is My Ability to Influence Future Events?

Unrealistic pessimists take the view "Whatever I do won't make a difference." Individuals who occupy this spot on the scale demonstrate Seligman's construct of learned helplessness. Failure to see how they can make a difference speaks volumes about their degree of personal efficacy, a critical dimension of one's resilience capacity (see Chapter 6). The school leader who is an unrealistic pessimist might view personal influence over the school budget in this way: "I have never been able to change the superintendent's mind. So why should I waste my time when it won't change anything?" Unrealistic pessimists succumb to deeper pessimism because their low sense of personal efficacy becomes a self-fulfilling prophecy.

Realistic pessimists acknowledge that they may be able to make a difference but conclude, "It isn't worth the effort on my part." A school leader who sees the world through the lens of the realistic pessimist might have this to say about the school budget problem: "The problems are real. And I guess I could go the extra mile and possibly help the superintendent see that my budget proposal is reasonable. But, quite frankly, it's too much work for so little reward." Realistic pessimists see the barriers but don't choose to do what it takes to remove them.

Realistic optimists believe that they can make a difference within the constraints imposed by reality. The school leader who approaches life from a realistic optimist orientation may see the budget problem as follows: "I give due credit to the negative aspects of this predicament with the budget. At the same time, I firmly believe that the goals likely can be achieved and that there are pathways to make it happen. I will search to find the pathways." Realistic optimists choose to frame the adversity in the language of challenges, and they seek to discover the controllable aspects of the adversity. They practice the wisdom found in the famous serenity prayer, summoning the courage to change the things they can and letting go of the things they can't change. As we discuss more fully in the next chapter, certain conditions do warrant letting go to the point of concluding, "This goal, under these circumstances, is not attainable." In general, though, realistic optimists have a strong sense of personal efficacy, and a key ingredient is the belief that they can make a positive difference in turning possibilities into reality.

Unrealistic optimists also hold a positive view of the future. They believe that they can influence the future. They believe it so much, in fact, that they strive for control over events without the resources to achieve them. A school leader who is an unrealistic optimist may take this position on the budget struggle: "I know things are tight financially. I also know that I can convince the superintendent that my budget proposal is feasible. I'm going to prevail on this. Just wait and see." Unrealistic optimists have trouble accepting that there are limits on what they can achieve. They often persist doggedly on tasks long after it is clear that the objective is unobtainable.

What Are My Expectations for Success?

Unrealistic pessimists can't see positive possibilities in negative situations. Believing that the worst-case outcomes will happen, they act accordingly, spending negative energy that drains their resilience account. A school leader who operates from an unrealistic pessimist framework may likely conclude, "I've no doubt what the chances are of this budget shortfall reversing itself during my tenure. Zero. I have lost sleep over this mess, but that doesn't change things. I have told the staff that they might as well brace themselves for the worst-case outcome." When unrealistic pessimists hold low expectations, they end up acting in a way that reinforces the negative possibilities.

Realistic pessimists hold low expectations that anything good will come out of their effort. Although they don't see the future as totally devoid of positive possibilities, they also don't assign much weight to the probability that a positive future will happen. So a combination of low expectations and a generally pessimistic view leads them to opt out of taking positive action on adverse circumstances. A school leader who is a realistic pessimist might forecast, "There is no sense wasting energy over trying to salvage the budget this year. There's not much of a possibility that effort on my part will make much difference. I need to spend my time elsewhere." Holding this position takes realistic pessimists out of the problem-solving mode and slots them into the victim mode, where they can avoid (in their own minds) any responsibility for raising the expectations of success.

Realistic optimists have positive expectations for the future. A school leader with this perspective might declare, "Good things can come from this budget quandary, but I will have to work at it to make the expectation reality. And the likelihood of success makes it worth my best effort." Sometimes realistic optimists entertain slightly optimistic illusions about what is possible. Research data show that optimistic illusions can produce greater resilience as long as these illusions don't dramatically distort reality. In other words, realistic optimists don't create false hope about what to expect. They may at times establish very high expectations, bordering on being unrealistic, but they also accept a lower threshold measure of acceptability for successful accomplishment.

Unrealistic optimists expect only the best. A school leader who is an unrealistic optimist might predict, "Best-case outcomes will happen; it will always work out." This belief structure can be counterproductive to resilience when unrealistic optimists become so driven by achieving the highest expectations that they create a demand for perfection by others as well as themselves. Most of the time perfection doesn't happen, and unrealistic optimists are stumped as to the reason why.

What Is the Focus of My Future Efforts?

When a storm hits, individuals choose the focus of their future efforts. This choice has significant implications for whether they invest positive energy or consume negative energy in response to the storm. Unrealistic pessimists choose to remain locked in the victim role. A school leader who sees life through this lens might remark, "There is no light at the end of the tunnel on this budget issue. The reality is that the budget is a catastrophe waiting to happen. I lie awake at night worrying about what's going to happen to our students when the budget crisis gets worse." In other words, unrealistic pessimists focus on the worst-case outcomes and waste valuable energy bemoaning adversity and their fate. This choice also relieves them, in their own mind, of any personal responsibility for how bad things are going to become for them.

Realistic pessimists have a reasonable grip on the reality of the situation. They choose to focus on all of the problems that the storm brings and to ignore the possibilities contained within the adversity. To illustrate the point, imagine a school leader who is a realistic pessimist commenting on the budget problems to her staff: "The problems we face this year are not the worst we've experienced, but they are serious. The bad outweighs the good and I don't see how the bad news is going to get fixed anytime soon. Prepare yourself for a rough ride through this budget crisis." Realistic pessimists acknowledge that the glass is half-full, but they focus on the problem of its being half-empty.

Realistic optimists have a data-based interpretation of the storm's seriousness. They see the problems but they focus on opportunities. A school leader who is a realistic optimist might observe, "I need to concentrate on how to act on the challenges of this budget shortfall in ways that move toward best-case outcomes, without focusing on perfection as the only acceptable measure of success." A reality-based focus has demonstrated payoffs for realistic optimists. According to Schneider (2001), "Dozens of studies of achievement motivation and self-regulation demonstrate that goal frames focused on positive states are functionally superior to goal frames focused on negative states. Positive focus leads to greater persistence, greater flexibility in strategies that reach a goal, greater creativity in solutions, better outcomes, and higher subjective well-being" (p. 256). Schneider goes on to say that a focus on hope and opportunity seeking can support both happiness and accomplishment without compromising realism, because people have considerable latitude in how they interact with the world they encounter.

Unrealistic optimists understand the reality of the situation, but they focus exclusively on achieving, at all costs, best-case outcomes. A school leader who operates out of the unrealistic optimist perspective might conclude, "Either I get all I need from the budget process, or all is lost. I am going to focus on securing 100 percent of my budget request. I won't settle for anything less." When the relentless focus on perfection doesn't produce the results that unrealistic optimists dreamed for, they consume a lot of resilience energy wallowing in their losses.

3

Optimism and Pessimism in Action

The pessimism–optimism scale presented in the previous chapter provides a conceptual framework to understand how optimists and pessimists approach life in general and adversity in particular. In this chapter, we move from concepts to practical application. First we describe a scenario facing a school leader and describe the actions taken by leaders at each point on the pessimism–optimism scale. Then we develop a profile of the realistic optimist, using experiences of those we interviewed to illustrate how realistic optimists respond to the six key questions outlined in Chapter 2.

Scenario: Current Reality

In the sixth year of the superintendent's tenure, relations with the board began to shift. The shift began when the board president decided to retire after 10 years of being president. The new board president was the former vice president and demonstrated zero leadership skills. He also felt he had a responsibility to give the board more freedom, because he believed that the former board president managed the board too tightly.

The so-called increase in freedom showed up as subtle things at first. No civility, no politeness, a definite contrast from previous board demeanor. Board members would rudely interrupt the superintendent and question personal motives. For example, when the superintendent gave the board different figures relative to budget calculations because of changing conditions at the state level, board members accused the administration of trying to trick them. Soon the board environment turned into a free-for-all where anyone, board members or community members, could say anything on any topic. For example, a board member bumped into a substitute bus driver at the grocery store. The bus driver complained that he didn't have rosters of all of the children on the bus. So at the next board meeting, the board member assailed the superintendent by saying, "I have concrete evidence that you don't care about the classified staff in this district. What do you intend to do about it?" The next day, a headline in the paper screamed, "Superintendent Accused of Treating Nonteaching Staff Unfairly."

The turning point in the superintendent's tenure in the district came when a major capital improvement project, the construction of new elementary and middle schools, was entered as a referendum to be voted on by the community in 90 days. What started out as an exciting project for the community turned into an incredibly divisive issue, separating those in favor of new schools from those primarily worried about higher taxes. And now the board is thick into the mess, making individual public statements for or against, well in advance of the referendum vote. All of this uproar puts the superintendent in a quandary: "How do I make sense of this predicament, and what do I do about it?" Presented here is the response to these questions, as framed by Superintendent Jeff Bloomer, the unrealistic pessimist; Superintendent Cheryl Ash, the realistic pessimist; Superintendent Juanita Cerruti, the unrealistic optimist; and Superintendent Buz MacKnight, the realistic optimist. Each of the superintendents decided to take a day away from the office, head to a cottage on the lake, and puzzle through what's going on now and what should go on from this point.

Bloomer: Unrealistic Pessimist

Superintendent Bloomer was the most negatively affected among the superintendents. The one-two punch of ugly board behavior and an upcoming voter rejection was too much to absorb at one time. This was Bloomer's first superintendency. He held a doctorate from the local university and had all of the requisite courses such as community–board relations and strategic planning. In fact, he aced both courses, and his strategic plan was singled out as the best in the class. So Bloomer entered the superintendent's job brimming with confidence. He believed strongly that if you lead a school district with your clear mission, vision, and values, others will follow if given the opportunity. He also believed that if you showed the board respect and treated them professionally, you could keep politics out of the mix when it comes to district decision making.

His outlook and expectations for how organizations could function effectively clearly didn't match what was going on right now. The board is out of control, thanks to feeble leadership by the new president. The community activists reject anything that the administration proposes. And now there is an insurmountable crisis that spells "f-i-r-e-d," to be stamped on the superintendent's forehead when the voters overwhelmingly say no at the polls. The board is at fault for refusing to monitor its own ranks. And within the administrative ranks, the community relations director is at fault for failing to be in touch with the divided sentiments in the community.

As Bloomer ponders the future, nothing about it has a glimmer of hope. He sees any changes in his recommendation to move ahead with the referendum as a show of weakness on his part. So he plans to plow ahead with the full project, certain that there is no chance of success. He knows that he can't make any difference in changing the community's mind. He knows that he has no influence over the board. And he knows that the end result will find his job on the chopping block in February. And who would want to hire a fired superintendent? At least he will go out knowing he acted with integrity in trying to do what's absolutely the best for students.

Ash: Realistic Pessimist

When it comes to the superintendency, Superintendent Ash has been around the block. Previously, she held the top job in two neighboring districts, logging 12 years in the superintendent's chair, before she accepted this position. Her current position has been the most challenging so far, but privately she would acknowledge that none of them has been very rewarding. Right now she faces her biggest challenge to her leadership. She saw it coming early on. The board started the politics dance, and she wasn't invited to the dance. At least she wasn't caught off-guard. Board politics, and even the community politics being stirred up by community activists, are all part of the reality of school district organizations. These forces have been barriers to success for her in her other head jobs.

Regarding the current storms, Ash saw these storms brewing when board leadership changed and the PTA elected a new leader, a union foreman in the paper mill. The biggest storm of all is the impending vote on the capital improvement project. And the prospects look grim. Ash commented to her husband at dinner last week that she probably contributed to the mess, because she didn't have to recommend to the board new construction of an elementary school and a middle school at the same time. But the primary blame rests squarely on the shoulders of the board. They are so divisive in their public comments. And the district community relations director didn't help matters by taking a two-week vacation just when the community was getting revved up.

As Ash looks to the future, not much good is going to come out of it. Sure, she could redouble her efforts to be out in the community, schedule visits at the local churches, and get on more agendas of the local civic service clubs. But what difference would it make? The effort required to turn things around just isn't worth it to Ash. The problem side of the equation is much heavier than the opportunity side. Early retirement never looked so good.

Cerruti: Unrealistic Optimist

Superintendent Cerruti is in her second year of the superintendent's job. She was the former high school principal in the district, and she was a star. When the superintendency became vacant, Cerruti jumped at the chance. And now she has an opportunity to show true leadership in the midst of crisis. As she sat beside the lake at her cottage mulling over the recent chain of events in the district, she saw rather quickly and clearly what was going on. On the one hand, she saw politics in action. No big deal. She learned as a high school principal that if you personally don't play politics, and you stick to the game plan, political activists can't harm your agenda. Sure, these politics are a little messier and more complex, but she can handle it all in her usual stellar fashion. Some people advised Cerruti to hold focus groups to take the temperature of community concerns. But Cerruti has confidence in her own intuition. She has relied on intuition before and it pulled her through other storms. Besides, women leaders know that intuition is a hallmark strength. She intuitively sees minimal risk in the threats posed by the rabble-rousers trying to defeat the referendum. The board politics is another sticky issue, but one that will resolve itself. The new board president is just testing his wings, and soon he will learn to fly in formation with the rest of the board. It is just a matter of time.

Looking to the immediate future, Cerruti remains wildly optimistic. She knows that she has strong credibility in the community, thanks in large part to her high-profile leadership as principal. She plans to call upon that strength to rally voters to a yes vote. And she has no doubt about a yes vote. As she told a colleague superintendent, "It's in the bag!" When the district business director posed the option of splitting the referendum into two parts, elementary school now and the middle school a couple of years later, Cerruti snapped, "That's not a perfect solution. That's a compromised solution. I expect the perfect solution to be the only one good enough for our students and our community. Full speed ahead."

MacKnight: Realistic Optimist

Buz MacKnight is a veteran superintendent, too. He has logged 10 years as superintendent in this district, and he previously served the district proudly as a generally successful high school football coach for five seasons. MacKnight is not new to stress and conflict. As a first-year coach, he pushed players too fast too soon; parents revolted, and several players quit in midseason. MacKnight learned from his mistakes and tempered his expectations to match the players' skill levels. Within a two-month period two years ago, MacKnight lost his high-school-aged son, who died in a tragic boat mishap, and his assistant principal to a protracted battle with cancer. So when the going gets tough related to school district issues, MacKnight works hard to keep things in perspective. For starters, he does not waste resilience points being "surprised" by the complexity, chaos, ambiguity, and politics of school systems. These elements are inherent in any organization. The key is to work within these variables, keeping your leadership eyes focused on what matters most. Granted, this immediate crisis related to the board being squirrelly and the community being contentious is nothing to ignore. But, as MacKnight sizes up the situation, the board "misconduct" is not permanent or pervasive. The new board president is flexing his muscle, but MacKnight coached the president's son in football and has a very trusting relationship with him. Superintendent MacKnight knows that in some ways he personally contributed to the problem by not meeting informally with the board president in anticipation of the current problems. He isn't overly worried about the community activists.

He hired a local firm to conduct opinion polls on community sentiment about the upcoming referendum, and the results were encouraging.

As MacKnight looks to the future, he believes that the board president is coachable, and MacKnight has already scheduled a series of breakfast meetings with him. The referendum is winnable, and MacKnight has drafted an alternative plan to place the elementary school portion of the capital improvement project on the upcoming ballot and to delay the middle school component for a couple of years. The opinion poll results showed that a majority of the community would "buy in" to this modification. Besides, MacKnight has learned the hard way that the perfect answer isn't always the best answer, considering all of the constraints standing in the way of perfection. MacKnight is optimistic about the outcome of these most immediate so-called district crises, and he is even more optimistic about the overall future of the district. But it is going to take a lot of hard work on his part, and it is by no means a done deal. Based on MacKnight's track record and his confidence in his leadership, he passionately believes that he can help make the district better than ever.

Scenario: Two Days After the Referendum Vote

In Superintendent Bloomer's view, things couldn't have turned out any worse. During the past 90 days, the board's conduct got progressively worse. Community activists got louder and uglier. The referendum failed, big-time. Today's editorial in the local paper called for Bloomer's resignation. Defeated and deflated, Superintendent Bloomer has little resilience capacity to fight back. He concludes, "I'm history here, and it doesn't look like I have a future anywhere else."

From Superintendent Ash's perspective, things turned out as anticipated. The board's behavior deteriorated. The referendum was defeated. Ash privately is grateful that she didn't spend much of her energy trying to alter the path of events. Her resilience capacity is low and she privately concedes, "Early retirement, here I come."

Superintendent Cerruti interpreted the outcome of the referendum vote as a huge professional and personal setback. She charged ahead in her typical style of making the best possible solution happen. Then it didn't. With her resilience capacity diminished, she laments to herself, "Whatever resilience reserves I have left I'm going to save for a district that wants the very best for the students, and it sure isn't this one."

For Superintendent MacKnight, things turned out well, just as he knew that they could. He altered his strategies over the past 90 days. He spent more time coaching the new board president on ways to keep the board hanging together. He dropped the middle school component of the referendum, reducing the price of the referendum by 60 percent. He logged a lot of evening hours with community groups. But the short-term costs on his part reaped huge dividends for the entire community. After the referendum vote, he was able to look into the TV cameras and publicly declare, "We did it."

Drawing strength from having come through this storm in good shape, MacKnight has a strengthened resilience capacity to face the future. But even if the referendum had been defeated, the superintendent would have chalked it up to lessons learned and continued his long-term positive outlook.

This brief scenario provides a quick review of how four superintendents holding distinct perspectives respond to adversity. As we argued earlier, the perspective of the realistic optimist provides the most likely chance to move ahead in the face of the storm.

Profile of Realistic Optimists

Realistic optimists interpret past and current reality differently than their colleagues who are at other points on the pessimism–optimism scale. In the scenario we just described, realistic optimists offer this analysis: "The lack of effective board leadership is the major source of the problem. But I have not done all that I could to help my new president be more effective. I may not be able to turn the situation around, but I need to try if we are to have any hope of passing the bond referendum." In the following sections, we enlarge this snapshot by showing how realistic optimists answer the six key questions linked to optimism.

What Assumptions Do I Hold About Reality?

This question focuses on reality at two levels. At the broadest level, realistic optimists hold assumptions about the reality of the world they live in. Several of the African Americans we interviewed spoke to assumptions about the reality of growing up in a segregated society. Ben Canada, associate executive director of the Texas Association of School Boards and a former superintendent in several states, talked about being raised in a community where certain things weren't granted to African Americans. In similar words, Gene Carter, Executive Director of the Association for Supervision and Curriculum Development (ASCD), said, "I grew up in a 'separate but equal' society, and one had to not just accept but deal with the circumstances as they were." Loucrecia Collins, a faculty member at the University of Alabama–Birmingham and former elementary principal, recalled the reality of life in West Point, Mississippi, where "you were born into certain classes, and whatever class you were born into, you were supposed to stay that way. The library was 'whites only,' so I didn't go to a public library until I was 13." Each person just mentioned refused to become whiners or victims of the reality. As we illustrate later in the chapter, they did not let their assumptions about the reality of the world they lived in deter them from maintaining a positive perspective about their world in the future.

Realistic optimists also don't back down from accepting realities about organizational life, even if it paints organizational life in less than glowing terms. Several educational leaders interviewed for this book discussed their assumptions about organizational reality. Michael Fullan, an internationally regarded authority in educational reform, told us, "Systems are not linear. Complex systems produce a fair amount of fragmentation and overload. You come to appreciate in an exquisite way what life and human beings in social systems are like. You know it is messy, so you take that as a given and aren't thrown by it. And then you are attracted to creating some patterns of goodness out of the messiness."

Peter Block, a consultant and author, spoke to the assumption that organizations are characterized by paradox. "Paradox is the reality that two opposite things are both true. How I deal with it is to accept the fact that they are both true. Transcend the paradox by acknowledging that they are both true, and they will be acting on me for the rest of my life. But you can't let the paradox paralyze you."

Paul Houston, AASA executive director, offered these observations and advice about the reality of paradox: "A core ability for any leader is to be able to hold competing thoughts in his or her mind and not be disquieted by that. A leader needs to say, 'Yeah, the world is confusing and contradictory and it is possible for two competing ideas to be right at the same time.' If I were running a program for leaders, I would make it a part of the core training to be comfortable with paradox. In order to teach it, I would create a course on dilemmas that people would have to wrestle with when there is no one right answer. I would have them grapple with the dilemma, talking about what they did and why they did it. Hopefully they would come to understand that they could have done it another way, and it would have been just as right or wrong. Then say it's OK, because that is what life is like in the real world."

Realistic optimists openly speak to the realities of organizational resistance when change is attempted. Larry Lezotte illustrated this point with an example: "Not long ago someone asked me how long my involvement with a given district transcends a change in leaders. This made me reflect, so on the plane ride home I got out a piece of paper and started making notes of places where I had ongoing relationships after a superintendent left. The answer is 'very few.' In fact, the reality is probably along the lines of 10 percent."

Yet, in the face of the harsh reality, Lezotte still believes in the possibilities of the future. Realistic optimists don't necessarily enter the profession comprehending all of the "realities" of organizational life. In some respects, they grow into it. As another bumper sticker says, "You live life forward and you understand it backward." Rubén Olivárez, superintendent of schools of the San Antonio Independent School District, commented that when he faced adversity in his job, he drew his strength from knowing that the issues were just the reality of what existed. "The things didn't scare me because of my experience in the past," he said.

Realistic optimists don't surprise easily. They have come to terms with the harsh reality that disruptions will happen. Linda Hanson, retired superintendent of Township High School District in Highland Park, Illinois, sees disruption as an opportunity. "I use disruption as a strategy, typically when I am planning and especially when I am planning with other people," she told us. "I will say to them, 'We're going to have some surprises in the course of this planning. And those surprises are going to be welcome, because they are going to give us brand-new perspectives. We'll tell each other when we get there, because we'll talk about them as one of the surprises. Plus, we will come away from the surprises a bit different because we had to make sense of it.' So my feeling is, build in the expectation of surprises up front, expect it, then use it as a strategy, and talk about it when it happens."

What Are the Causes of the Current Adversity, Including My Own Contribution?

Realistic optimists seek accurate data to understand "what's really going on around here?" Lynne Shain, an assistant superintendent in the West-port, Connecticut, School District, described her basic strategy: "When I am facing a challenge, I typically talk to people, asking questions to help me figure out where I am going to go. So if there is a crisis and I need to act, I first make sure that I have it [the reality] clearly in my mind and that I have tested the recommendations with a number of people. Then I can calmly go out with what I am going to do."

Realistic optimists also want to know how they contributed to the problem. Several school leaders we interviewed courageously pointed to situations where they did take action and, upon reflection and soul-searching, were wrong. Canada volunteered an example of making a costly mistake that contributed to tension with the school board.

"As superintendent in Portland," he said, "I gave a state of the school district address. I had analyzed the state of the school district in terms of what needed to be done. I then devised a plan, but I didn't share it with the school board before I went public with the media in full attendance. And while the school board liked the idea that I was taking charge, they did not like—and rightfully so—the fact that I was sharing information in a public forum before they had an opportunity to think about and devise a response. And when I was almost at the end of my address, I looked over at my school board, and I could see in their faces that I had made a mistake."

Immediately after the address, reporters hammered the board with questions, such as "How can we afford to do this?" and "Do you agree with the superintendent?" The board struggled to articulate a coherent response on short notice and without preparation. Although Canada recovered from his mistake, his actions were costly in the short run, and he had to work hard to regain the support of the board.

Realistic optimists know that mistakes can be costly. In assessing risks, however, they also know the price paid for inaction during times of adversity. As Herman Gaither, superintendent of schools in Beaufort County, South Carolina, summed up the sentiments of many of those we talked with, "If you are going to wait until you get it right, you will never do anything." And Carter offered this perspective: "In many institutional contexts, leaders manifest a sort of behavior that if a person makes a mistake, there are penalties to pay. I have sort of reversed that. We grow from the mistakes we make. I constantly try to keep in my mind a quote attributed to Albert Einstein: 'I haven't failed. I found 10,000 ways that don't work.' That is part of how I have tried to provide some sense of leadership: living out my beliefs and values."

Block told us that as he works with groups across the world, he challenges them to see how they have contributed to the adversity. "When I ask people how they contribute to the problem, and they say they can't think of anything, I tell them, 'That is precisely how you contribute to the problem. You want to take the innocent role, the moral high road.' "

Then Block, in his typical style, challenges them further, "Grow up, you are human, you're guilty [of contributing to the problem]." He then counsels leaders, "Accept your humanity. Don't try to be more than you are."

What Are the Risks Posed by the Adversity?

Realistic optimists work hard to accurately assess the risks posed by the adversity because they are committed to making informed judgments about what to do. They don't deny or dismiss the level of threat. Vince Ferrandino, executive director of the National Association of Elementary School Principals, recalled a major storm during his tenure as education commissioner in Connecticut. His adversity centered on efforts to desegregate the public schools.

"I was charged by the governor to come up with a plan," he said. "It was a very complex issue, and we found ourselves as state officials working at odds with the attorney general who was bound by duty to defend the state in the *Sheff v. O'Neill* case. I was opposed on the issue and quite frankly told them, 'We've made some efforts here to equalize education, but it hasn't made a difference.' This wasn't what the attorney general wanted to hear, but that was the way it was.

"Things began to heat up real quickly. I received communications from a chapter of the Klan and other groups opposed to the desegregation plan. The threatening nature of these communications resulted in police surveillance of my home. And on a couple of occasions, the police provided an escort from the town meeting."

Ferrandino, in the face of crisis conditions, didn't flinch. "I had a strong belief in what I was doing . . . in providing equal education. It was at the core of my belief system."

Realistic optimists try very hard to gather accurate information to fully understand past and present reality. They don't duck the fact that they, too, have contributed to the reality. But a realistic interpretation of what's happening isn't enough. School leaders also need to have an accurate interpretation of future possibilities growing out of adversity.

What Is My Ability to Influence Future Events?

Realistic optimists answer this question as follows: "I can make a difference within the constraints posed by reality. The goals likely can be achieved, despite the adversity I face, and I will seek the path to make it happen." At the same time, realistic optimists give due credit to the negative aspects of the adversity. They choose to frame the adversity in the language of challenges and try to discover the controllable aspects of the adversity. Carter commented on his youth as an African American, saying, "You had to look beyond the reality of the present. You had to look to the future and believe that it could be different. I always knew conditions would change; it was just a matter of how soon they would change. So I was not rooted in what was. I was rooted in how I would prepare myself for what could be."

Then Carter smiled as he recalled this story: "I always had a part-time job. I worked in a men's clothing store after school and assisted the tailor. The owner of the store was fond of me. One day he asked me what I wanted to do when I grew up. It was not the routine at the time for kids like me in the community to go on to college. I said very proudly, 'That's not even a question I need to grapple with. I'm going to do the same kinds of things you do. I am going to be successful.' As time passed, I kept in contact with him. When I would return home in the summer, we would chat, and he would want to know how I was doing. He died before I finished undergraduate school, but I always believed that *he* always believed that I would make it."

Collins responded this way to the reality of growing up in West Point. "I didn't buy into that [the limitations of class and race]. My boundaries were so much more expansive than what I saw. I remember seeing people on TV go to big offices and my daddy didn't go to an office. He had a lunch pail and he went to the lumber mill." She added that these images of possibilities "spurred me on to believe that I could have whatever I wanted to have in life. There were no boundaries."

Collins's comments are reflective of the sentiments shared by many of the realistic optimists whom we interviewed. They have a strong sense of personal efficacy, and a key ingredient is the belief that they can make a positive difference in turning possibilities into reality.

What Are My Expectations for Success?

A realistic optimist responds, "Good things may happen, but I will have to work at it. So I will do whatever is within my influence to make the expectations reality. And the likelihood of success is worth the effort." Consider the example of Loucrecia Collins. As a very young single mother, Collins wanted an advanced education so she could provide adequately for her children. When she eventually started on her doctoral degree, she would not sacrifice her role as mother at the expense of education. She expected that she could do it all. "I wanted to be Supermom. I was the band booster mom, a Girl Scout leader, and drove children to the movies on the weekend. I was also a full-time teacher and going to school two or three nights a week. There was zilch money. I'm telling you, it was some tough times. But I just knew and expected that I could get through this education and have a better life and foundation for my children. I was not going to be a single mom on welfare. That was not going to happen to me. I was not going to be a statistic."

Realistic optimists like Collins have a tendency to set their sights a bit too high. Gaither describes a conscious strategy to aim a little high: "I'm the push-forward guy. I've got to have the backfillers. So when I go out and say, 'We're going to do this, this and this,' I know we're going to push it out to the edge. If I want to get to 10, then I've got to say, 'Let's shoot for 20.' And then realistically we end up at 10. And everybody makes progress. But if you don't push the edges of the envelope, you stay inside the same confines."

The prevailing research data show that optimistic illusions can produce greater resilience as long as these illusions don't distort the reality of the situation. In other words, realistic optimists don't create false hope about what to expect. They may at times establish very high expectations, bordering on being unrealistic, but, like Gaither, they also accept a lower threshold of acceptability for successful accomplishment.

What Will Be the Focus of My Efforts?

When a storm hits, individuals must accept that they alone must choose the focus of their efforts. This choice has significant implications whether they *invest* positive energy or *consume* negative energy in response to the storm. Realistic optimists seek as much data as possible so that they can interpret the seriousness of the storm. They want to understand the problems as well as the opportunities. As we said earlier, they are more aggressive than pessimists in searching for meaning in the negative aspects of adversity. By understanding and anticipating the possibilities of negative outcomes, realistic optimists approach the positive outcomes with a more realistic perspective. They place their emphasis on the positive, concentrating on how to act on the challenges in ways that move toward best-case outcomes, in contrast to unrealistic optimists who will settle only for perfection. Gaither reflected the view of many school leaders we interviewed on the topic of staying focused on what matters most: "I took the superintendency because I really wanted an opportunity to find out if, given the reality of the circumstances and given an extended period of time, we could produce a significantly different result for our school district. The leadership has to be focused on something that's out there that's going to improve the kind of education we are offering our kids."

Gaither, like other realistic optimists, holds high expectations for the future and, at the same time, understands that achieving something less is not total failure. "My beliefs are not intended to say that a program is going to solve all of our problems. But the goals we have are goals that live inside the heart, soul, and mind of the people who make up the institution." At a personal level, school leaders who are realistic optimists have goals, driven by their core values, that live inside their heart, soul, and mind. They find ways to work within the realities of the human condition and the realities of the organization to achieve these goals. They will not be denied.

When Giving Up Is a Strength

Most of us have heard the common refrain "Never give up. Winners don't quit and quitters don't win." And who wants to be labeled a loser or a quitter? This logic trap presumes that if you ever quit in your efforts to win or stay the course you get branded negatively. And brands tend to be rather permanent. In reality, each of us, even the most ardent, die-hard realistic optimists among us, encounter life experiences during which we simply cannot reach our goal. What then? Do we just give up and join the ranks of the defeated? To spotlight the way out of this conundrum, Carver and Scheier (2003) emphasize the difference between giving up effort and giving up commitment to the larger goal. The researchers frame their argument in terms of the principle of "hierarchicality among the goal values of the self" (p. 90). The authors elaborate:

> We believe that goals provide the structure that defines people's lives. The goals of the self take a variety of forms. Some are concrete (e.g., taking out the garbage); others are more abstract and ephemeral (e.g., being a good parent). What makes one goal matter more than another? Generally speaking, the higher in the hierarchy a goal is, the more important it is (the more central to the overall self). Concrete action goals acquire importance from the fact that attaining them serves the attainment of more abstract goals. The stronger the link between a concrete goal and the deepest values of the self, the more important is that concrete goal. (p. 90)

Applying these thoughts to our superintendent scenarios, the capital improvement project was primarily about the higher-order goal of providing adequate facilities to a growing student population. The concrete action goal was to pass a bond referendum for a new elementary and new middle school. Cerruti, the wild-eyed optimist, equated the passage of the referendum with the higher-order goal. She wanted perfection or nothing. She refused to give up. On the other hand, MacKnight sought an alternative pathway to achieve the higher-order goal of adequate facilities. He proposed a staggered referendum time line: first the elementary school and then the middle school. In one sense, he did give up. He gave up on going down the original path when he foresaw a dead end. He crafted an alternative path to achieve the higher-order goal of meeting the students' needs for long-term facilities.

Sometimes giving up means giving up on goals that are very much at the core of self. In Patterson's (2000) research on the superintendency, some of the superintendents gave up the goal of being a successful superintendent and shifted their career path. Such disengagement of goals was deliberately chosen in the spirit of achieving a higher-order self-goal of strengthening the core of personal efficacy, which we describe in Chapter 6. Wise choices within this category of giving up develop over time into a resilience strength. We should emphasize, however, that the ability to make wise choices depends heavily on an individual's ability to be very clear about the hierarchy of personal values most important to defining self. For example, some people choose immediate goals such as comfort (through eating junk food) over the long-term goals of good health that could be achieved through healthier eating habits. However, most people would probably agree that good health is central to their life's goals.

Another form of giving up is what Carver and Scheier (2003) term "giving up in lifespan development." The authors note several ways in which life span goals get rendered unattainable. One way is that biological resources available to a person have a period of growth and decline over the life span. Recall the example of Roland Barth discussing problems with his back. Earlier in his life, he could choose, from a value-added perspective, hauling firewood or skiing. Now his choices have become more loss based. Barth gave up on his ability to haul firewood (a loss) and replaced it with getting his nephews to help him.

As noted earlier, giving up presents a conundrum. When does giving up become a strength? Carver and Scheier respond:

> The problem is how to know when something is truly unattainable (or not worth the effort required to attain it). In truth, whenever the issue arises, it is impossible to be certain of the answer. To persevere may turn out to be glorious stupidity. To give up may turn out to be a tragic loss. The well-known serenity prayer asks for 'the wisdom to know the difference' between these cases. Whether the answer comes from a divinity or from a lifetime of experience, the ability to choose wisely (or at least believe that one has chosen wisely) and follow one's choice fully is also an important strength. (p. 95)

At the beginning of this chapter, we defined *realistic optimism* as the ability to maintain a positive outlook in the face of adversity, without denying reality and the constraints posed by reality. Throughout this chapter, we have described a framework to help you, in the words of Carver and Scheier, choose wisely. When adversity strikes, how you choose to interpret current and past reality and how you choose to interpret future possibilities makes all the difference in how you call upon your resilience capacity to move through the storm stronger than ever.

4

BE CLEAR ABOUT
WHAT MATTERS MOST

Throughout our interviews with educational leaders in preparation for this book, the most dominant theme cutting across all of our conversations was the theme of *personal values*. Those we interviewed repeatedly and passionately told us that the process of privately clarifying, publicly articulating, and consciously acting on their personal values is the greatest source of strength to help them navigate through the storms of life and come out on the other side stronger than before. The purpose of this chapter and Chapter 5 is to demonstrate how you can draw upon your own personal values to build personal resilience in the face of adversity.

Hierarchy of Values

Educational leaders, along with leaders in most professions, have a deserved reputation for spewing forth a barrage of well-intentioned slogans that attempt to convey meaning but fail miserably in practice. No wonder people tune out when school leaders start chirping about mission, vision, and values. Many times school leaders themselves aren't clear about what they mean. This lack of clarity inevitably creates even greater confusion in the minds of those receiving the message. Especially in times of adversity, people need leaders to provide clear direction anchored in clearly understood values. These personal values are nested in layers to create a hierarchy that portrays what matters most to you (Figure 4.1).

At the top of this hierarchy sit your deeply held *core* values. One component of core values is the theme of universal ethical principles. Philosophers and theologians throughout recorded history have debated the meaning of ethics. We have neither the motivation nor

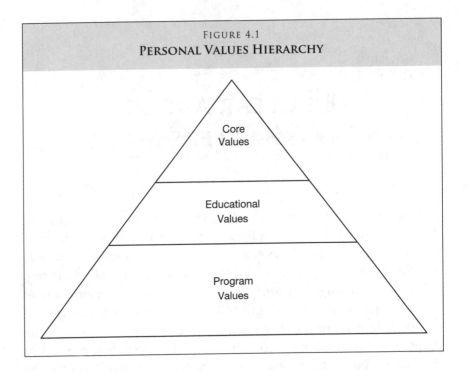

FIGURE 4.1
PERSONAL VALUES HIERARCHY

Core
Values

Educational
Values

Program
Values

the expertise to enter the debate. For our purposes, we refer to ethics as the highest-order personal values about what is right and wrong. Ethical values reflect a set of universal principles that transcend the mission, vision, and values of any particular organization. Fullan (2002) refers to this concept as "moral purpose," the social responsibility to others and the environment. At a global level, an example of a document articulating a set of universal values about moral purpose is the United Nations' Universal Declaration of Human Rights. The declaration contains 30 articles to serve as a common standard for defining moral purpose for all peoples and nations. At a personal level, your ethical principles consist of themes such as trustworthiness, responsibility, and caring. The source of your ethical principles about right and wrong can be as general as the belief in the Golden Rule or as specific as the doctrine of a religious faith. In either case, the ethical person is guided by universal principles, seeking to help others and refraining from causing harm to others.

A second component of core values consists of individualized values that help define your character. One person may hold a bedrock core value of loving others, with family always coming first. Another person may have a core value of winning at all costs. In both cases, the core individualized values help define the person's character. We asked each of the 25 educators whom we interviewed a common question: "In the face of adversity, how do you remain focused on being a value-driven, not event-driven, leader?" The respondents were uniform in their commitment to core ethical values. Gerrita Postlewait is clear about her core: "I know my life is about improving the quality of human life for others. That's what I am on this earth for."

Paul Houston added, "I find that when I am really connected to my beliefs in a powerful way, I have a lot more personal power about what I am doing. There is a lot more peace, which allows you to go through things with a different view than when you face adversity and you aren't steady on your feet." He then conveyed his deep respect for those superintendents who leave well-functioning school districts to go to an urban setting because, as they have told him, "These other kids need me more."

Ben Canada spoke softly and passionately about the importance of one's moral compass. "If you truly believe in yourself and have high moral values, your moral compass is pointed in the right direction." He recalled a concrete example that gave him strength and affirmation about living a life anchored in core ethical values.

"When I was in Atlanta," Canada said, "one of the students had to introduce me. She said, 'I want to introduce you to a man who is truthful to himself, to us, and to others, and a person who lives those convictions without saying them. And I can say to you that Dr. Canada is a person of faith without him ever saying what religion he believes in, that he goes to church, that he tries to live and do what is right. But simply by his actions, in the way he talks to people, the way he seeks input from others, and the way he challenges when one is trying to do that which is wrong. And he rewards people when they're really trying to do the right thing that's morally right.' "

Canada was deeply moved by the introduction. "That to me was one of the best introductions that one could have given to me because it was the essence of who I try to be."

For Gene Carter, family values stood prominent in his mind. "In trying to act out my core values, I was never too busy to listen to my kids," he told us. "I always had dinner with my family because I felt it was important, especially when they were young. We also had a family council, and each person had a vote. As an example, when I was selected to be superintendent in Norfolk, we sat down and discussed the pros and cons. The consensus was that I should accept the Norfolk job. We did the same thing when I accepted this position at ASCD."

All the leaders we interviewed made clear that core values, ethical principles about right and wrong, as well as individualized core values that help define character, stood at the top of their Personal Values Hierarchy.

Just beneath the core values level in the hierarchy are key *educational* values. Just as core values express your overall belief about what is important in life, certain professional values express your belief about what matters most in your work environment. One of the most consistent professional values emerging from our interviews is the central principle of student learning. Linda Hanson looked back on her career and contrasted what life was like before and after her placement of student learning at the heart of her educational values.

"I feel that I can almost see two parts of my career. There was a part when I was a very young administrator where I was not grounded in the philosophy that guided everything I did. And I was more event-driven. And the reason I was event-driven is because I really was not totally grounded in what I thought [about teaching and learning]. And I find when I talk to other administrators, those who are not well grounded in knowing what they believe about teaching and learning are having a much more difficult time."

Postlewait made a similar observation about being grounded: "In my previous superintendency, I did not focus enough on my passion of teaching and learning. I think the reason is that I was not mature enough or wise enough to know how to handle all of the information and decisions that were coming to the superintendent's desk in a way that maximized the talents of other people and that carved out time for my central passion of teaching and learning."

Michael Fullan reinforced Postlewait's belief in a leader needing to focus on the educational value of student learning. In his interview, he described efforts of the Chicago School District to divide the schools into 24 clusters, each headed by an area instructional officer (AIO). "The district began hiring people into those positions who had a strong track record for instruction. Then they appointed a management director in each cluster who reports to the AIO. The management director handled the day-to-day issues, and the AIO relentlessly focused on instruction."

Rubén Olivárez articulated several key values that guided his actions, concluding that the overriding value was that the teacher is the program. Tom Sergiovanni, a professor of educational administration and supervision at Trinity University and a scholar in educational leadership, supported this point during his interview. School leaders need to be clear about what is at the center and what's at the periphery of values, he said. "If you put accountability at the center, it is not going to work. You need to put learning and teaching at the center and then some magic happens." Sergiovanni tries to live his professional life accordingly. "One virtue I have is focus, to be able to have a razor-sharp focus on having a handful of things that are really important to me, and I try not to dilute what I'm doing across the whole spectrum of the rainbow."

Lynne Shain wondered aloud whether superintendents, by virtue of their jobs, become forced to be more event-driven than value-driven. "In today's superintendency, I think the superintendents are much more vulnerable whereas someone in my position [assistant superintendent] is better able to be the chief advocate for teaching and learning." Regardless of who the chief advocate is, Shain is clear about what is most important in a school district: "We need to keep our eye on our north star, and our north star is teaching."

Interviewees described many examples of their struggles to lead in the face of adversity. And in the midst of these struggles, these educational leaders described how they worked relentlessly to stay focused professionally on what matters most. As we will discuss in more depth later, these challenges increase when educators are confronted with competing values in the values hierarchy.

The third level in the values hierarchy consists of *program* values that give meaning and direction to specific initiatives in an organization. For example, what are the values you hold for specific educational initiatives occurring on your watch as school leader? What do you value in areas such as elementary reading, professional development, or student assessment? What do you value regarding shared decision making, parent involvement, and equitable learning opportunities irrespective of race, gender, class, and other conditions? What do you value that steers you through the tough times and gives you courage to act on your convictions? The purpose of raising questions like these is not to imply there is one right answer to the questions. Our purpose is to amplify the importance that values play, irrespective of your specific answers, in giving meaning and direction to the program initiatives in your organization. Suppose, for example, that you are considering sending some of your staff members to a professional development session. As you contemplate which activities to choose, suppose that your school or district has a tight budget, and you must make difficult choices about the most appropriate investment of scarce professional development funds. Unless you are clear about your program values, you have no solid basis to help determine which events to undertake.

Key program values also help you select among a wide variety of commercial programs on an educational topic. In the area of elementary mathematics instruction, for example, school districts have numerous products to choose from, including the following:

- Everyday Math
- Math Trailblazers
- Investigations
- TERC Math
- Saxon Math

Each of these programs is built on certain program values about teaching and learning mathematics. If you are clear on your own program values about teaching and learning mathematics, you make mathematics program decisions in a value-driven, not an event-driven, way.

The Power of Competing Values

The Personal Values Hierarchy shown in Figure 4.1 helps label and understand the distinctions among the three levels of values. In the real world of organizational leadership, it is rather straightforward to develop, articulate, and embrace values at each level. The proverbial rub comes when competing values jockey for position on the values hierarchy. Badaracco (1997) refers to this as *defining moments* for leaders, conditions where leaders are caught in a conflict between right and right. Resolving the defining moment's conflicts requires skills not listed on job descriptions. Consider the following illustration on a national scale that had profound and far-reaching consequences.

On February 1, 2003, the space shuttle *Columbia* disintegrated on its return to Earth, ending seven lives and prompting an independent investigation board to conclude that the National Aeronautics and Space Administration's (NASA) competing values were as much responsible for the tragedy as any technical problems uncovered. The NASA leaders publicly embraced two important values related to organizational culture: a culture of safety and a culture of high performance.

NASA leaders proclaimed that the value related to safety was at the top of their values hierarchy. In initial briefings to the investigation board, NASA officials espoused a risk-free philosophy. They went so far as to say that NASA valued doing whatever it takes to ensure the safety of the crew. In other words, they valued safety at all costs. What the investigation board found was that the leaders engaged in personnel cutbacks, coupled with demands to work evenings and weekends, to meet the NASA mission's value of successful, on-time launches. Among competing values, NASA leaders valued efficiency more than they did safety. The investigation board concluded that NASA managers were obsessed with making the over-budget and behind-schedule International Space Station credible to the White House and Congress. As one of the engineers commented during the board investigation, "It just doesn't make any sense to me why *at all costs* we were marching to scheduled launch dates." The investigation board did not take issue with either of the values embraced by NASA leaders. Adherence to values of high performance and safety is laudable. What concerned the board was that NASA officials held the value of high performance above all others, creating competition for energy, talent, and other resources. The consequences speak for themselves.

This real-life example dramatically highlights what happens when two competing values vie for placement in the Personal Values Hierarchy. Some people would argue that educators don't put lives on the line in the same way that NASA does. However, we do put our students' educational lives and their educational future on the line every day. And in today's environment laced with adversity, how do you sort out what matters most? Larry Lezotte offered one perspective during his interview.

"I think one of the things you ought to do as you are appointed to a leadership position," he said, "is to go off to your version of Walden Pond and decide which hills you are willing to die on. And that becomes your center. They are the things you care most about. The people who bounce back when they are hammered by adversity did not lose that center. They were centered on core values that were deep in them. They would rather die organizationally or career-wise than compromise that. They articulate the core values to the critical mass around them. As they do this, the core values tend to grow, as an organic thing, and when that happens, they have the capacity to take heavy weather and keep coming back."

Two educational leaders we interviewed gave an example of having to terminate an employee as a real-life example of competing values. Charles Fowler, an educational consultant and former superintendent of schools in several states, described it this way: "Difficult as it may be, I've had to fire a number of people in 35 years and always agonized over that. I thought, 'Who are you to take food from the table of this family?' or whatever the implication was. I agonized over that. In the final analysis, I always felt it was for the better good of the school district and a lot of kids. It was also for the better good of the individual. Why keep a person in a nonproductive setting? And if they are not able to realize that, then maybe ultimately they will. So, I think using a value-driven position gives you a comfort and makes the difference."

Hanson experienced comparable anguish in her coming to terms with firing an employee. "I had to fire a teacher with three kids," she said. "I anguished about putting a man out in the street with three little girls. Then I put myself in the students' role and thought, 'OK what's more important, to put a man out in the street with three little girls or all of the kids (he had been here for a long time) who had him and were not getting an education?' How do you balance one against the other? And I thought that the ultimate responsibility was to all the students coming through the class and not to him and his three children. Now, luckily he did find another job, and he was probably better suited for it, but I didn't know if he would find another job."

"You have no choice but to weigh what is the higher-level purpose," she added. "You also have to have faith in yourself and the tenacity to keep moving through it with the belief that it will be the right thing."

Many of the school leaders we interviewed talked at length about facing competing values and having to agonize over what matters most within the Personal Values Hierarchy. The leaders also found many ways to create "and" thinking rather than "either-or" thinking. In other words, when faced with competing values, how can you honor the demands placed on you and, at the same time, be true to the values that matter most?

Here's how Phil Schlechty approached "and" thinking in Louisville: "When I came to Louisville in 1984, I came here at the behest of the business community to improve the quality of teaching. It didn't take me long to figure out there were two sets of competing needs reflected in the business community. One group of businesspeople really wanted the schools to improve. The other group wanted the *reputation* of the schools to improve and they would support school improvement if they had to in order to get their agenda to happen. What I had to recognize was that it wasn't enough for me to work on the improvement of schools. I also had to show them, and relatively quickly, how to improve the reputation of the schools. I spent a lot of time with the newspaper reporters, such as the *New York Times,* creating the impression that the schools were 'on the road' long before they were actually getting better. So I had to deal with both sets of values. If I had done nothing but focus on improving teaching and learning, I would not have been able to sustain the activity."

Shain provided another glimpse into how to pursue "and" thinking. "We had a lot of pressure that started five years ago," she told us. "Our district was kind of in the middle or the lower end of our Educational Reference Group [ERG]. A new superintendent took over. He felt that in order to be viable in terms of the budget process, we needed to get our scores up. The scores weren't terrible, but they weren't in the top three or four in the ERG, and we needed to do something about that. This is very difficult for me because, previously, I was able to say, 'Well, our curriculum . . . is a rich curriculum.' Our board had always said, 'Build a rich curriculum, and don't become a test prep district.' The board changed, the superintendent changed, and they felt compelled to say, 'Get your test scores up,' because [the subject of test scores] was being used in the budget battles. And so I needed to be able to explain that and to help faculty deal with this in a way that made them realize that we'd keep true to our core values and still do better on these tests if we would embed the test material in our curriculum. The challenge to me was to figure out a way to deal with the issue but stay true to the core values, and the method was embedding test content in the curriculum."

When the battle lines are drawn and you must choose among competing, conflicting values, it helps to have a sounding board for you to expose your own frustrations about value conflicts. According to Dennis Sparks, executive director of the National Staff Development Council, "My experience is that, for most of us, it is critically important to have someone to talk to, to reveal our feelings and thoughts in a most honest and direct way. I am not talking necessarily about psychotherapy. I am talking about getting together with colleagues and moving beyond the superficial façade of bus schedules or just complaining, to the point of making ourselves vulnerable. My experience has been that when we take that risk, more often than not other people reveal themselves to us and we begin talking in different kinds of ways. Through this, we begin to see how we resolve these value conflicts."

Sparks acknowledged that there have been many times in his life when values were in tension with each other. "On the one hand, I value freely speaking my mind, but I also value economic security. So sometimes my values are in conflict." When this happened, Sparks turned to his own values hierarchy, and, if core values were at stake, he knew what he needed to do. "There are times when I don't want to live a divided self. So I speak up at all costs."

Our view is consistent with the position taken by Sparks. When you find yourself faced with adversity and the tension caused by competing values, turn to the Personal Values Hierarchy. Core values come first, even if you must sacrifice some key professional values along the way. As we illustrate in the next chapter, sometimes these tough choices in adverse times carry a high price, personally and professionally. Realistically, though, that's what the Personal Values Hierarchy is all about: making tough choices under tough circumstances regarding what matters most to us.

5

ACT ON THE COURAGE OF
YOUR CONVICTIONS

Core values reflect the heart and soul of leaders. Imagine, for instance, a newly appointed school leader who stands before all employees and declares a firm commitment to the following core values: communication, respect, excellence, and integrity. These are core values that any employee would appreciate in a leader. This situation actually happened in the year 2000 at the annual meeting of a highly respected organization. The leader was the CEO of Enron Corporation. What was professed is not what was enacted by the leaders. The rest of the story is history that we can learn from. As one researcher warned:

> I've spent the last 10 years helping companies develop and refine their corporate values, and what I've seen isn't pretty. Most value statements are bland, toothless, or just plain dishonest. And far from being harmless, as some executives assume, they're often highly destructive. Empty value statements create cynical and dispirited employees, alienate customers, and undermine managerial credibility. (Lencioni, 2002, p. 5)

Consciously Construct Your Values

As we discussed in Chapter 4, personal values contribute heavily to shaping your resilience capacity. Unfortunately, many times school leaders are not only unclear to others about their personal values but also unclear to themselves. Chuck Schwahn, a consultant and former superintendent of the Eagle County School District in Colorado, commented during our interview that he was surprised at times by the reality that superintendents had not sufficiently reflected on the topic of core values.

"When I ask superintendents about their own core values, I discover that people haven't done their own work on this topic," Schwahn said. "People haven't been intentional about these things. They need to make the connection between their own core values and how they connect to their work. Probably that is the biggest strength of resilience—to have all of these things in your personal life so aligned that it is not like 'I am going to my job now.' But many of us go through our life unintentionally, without stopping and reflecting. A line by Steven Covey has heavily influenced my life: 'If it is important it should be intentional.'"

Dennis Sparks made a similar observation, based on his work with educators across the world: "Most of us go about our daily life without reflecting on what we intend and what we value." This pattern takes a huge toll on your resilience capacity. If you aren't clear about what matters most to you, then you drain your energy and decrease your efficacy. In contrast, as those we interviewed underscored repeatedly, you strengthen your resilience when you anchor yourself in a set of core values, clearly understood by you and clearly articulated to others. Although we readily acknowledge that there is no single recipe for constructing core values that works best for everyone, we draw upon the writing and experience of Patterson (2003) to outline a four-step process as one way to develop core values.

Step 1: State the Core Value

The core value process begins with a simple sentence stem describing what you care deeply about at a given level in the core values hierarchy. This statement may describe a core ethical principle such as trust, a core professional value such as student achievement, or a core program value such as the topic of character education.

To illustrate Step 1, we select a specific category from each of two dimensions of resilience capacity introduced in Chapter 1: personal efficacy and personal energy.

- *Personal efficacy:* I value personally making a difference in the lives of students.
- *Personal energy:* I value using my physical energy productively to achieve my goals.

By constructing core values in each of these areas, you take an important first step toward strengthened resilience. You declare what matters most to you. This helps move you from an event-driven mentality of chasing the latest leadership fads to a value-driven system for sorting out how you will spend the currency in your resilience bank account. When you state in writing what you value, you push yourself to make clear what previously may have been cloudy in your mind.

Step 2: Add the Power of *I Will* Statements

To give added clarity and specificity to your core belief, a second step is to add the power of *will* to the value statements. In this context, we are using the term *will* in two ways. We mean the will, or determination, to see the value come alive in daily practice. Without the will, value statements sit as idle commitments with no force of energy propelling the values into action. We also use the term to reflect what you will do to act on the value. Just as the *I value* statements are a public disclosure of what you care most about, the *I will* statements are a public declaration of what you can expect from yourself and what others can expect from you because of what you say you value. Here are examples of *I will* statements applied to the same two categories:

Personal efficacy: I value personally making a difference in the lives of students. Therefore, I will

- Organize my time so that I focus first on students' needs;
- Create forums so I can listen carefully to students talking about their needs;
- Make sure that my career path keeps me in a role that serves students.

Personal energy: I value using my physical energy productively to achieve my goals. Therefore, I will

- Practice healthy eating on a regular basis;
- Allow time for recovery after periods of strenuous physical demands;
- Get enough sleep so that I am physically energized the next day.

The power of will stems initially from becoming clear and public about what you will do to act on your value. For many leaders, the will is strengthened by taking the risky step of saying to the world, "This is what you can expect from me." Once you make clear what your values are, your integrity is on the line regarding your follow-through with promised actions. Otherwise, people will say that you don't "walk the talk."

Step 3: Take Action Consistent with Your Values

Resilience accounts start to shrink when the best of intentions don't materialize into results. Suppose you struggle with the personal adversity of being overweight, so you make a typical New Year's resolution: "I value losing weight so I can be more healthy. Therefore, I will enroll in a weight-loss program next week." The intentions are honorable, and the will is declared. But a large percentage of individuals making such resolutions don't sustain the needed actions over time, which initiates the cycle of feeling less efficacious, less energetic, and less certain about the relative importance of weight loss among competing personal values in your core values hierarchy.

Actions that are consistent with your values produce small wins for you. Losing six pounds in a month, for example, gives you a greater sense of efficacy and a stronger belief that you can reach your goal. This success encourages you to continue with the actions that worked over the past month. You are buoyed by tangible evidence that your comfort-food sacrifices were worth the price paid.

The same patterns apply to the professional lives of leaders who follow through with their commitments in the form of *I value; therefore, I will* statements. Returning to the earlier examples of personal efficacy and personal energy, let's insert the action step into the equation: strength = value + will + action.

Personal efficacy: I value making a difference in the lives of students. Therefore, I will

- Organize my time so that I focus first on students' needs;
- Create forums so I can listen carefully to students talking about their needs;

• Make sure that my career path keeps me in a role that serves students.

And then I took the following actions:

• Organized my daily schedule so I am in classrooms observing, teaching, and learning for at least an hour a day;
• Met with the Student Council on a regular basis each month to hear what's on students' minds;
• Declined an invitation to apply for a central office position.

Personal energy: I value using my physical energy productively to achieve my goals. Therefore, I will

• Practice healthy eating on a regular basis;
• Allow time for recovery after periods of strenuous physical demands;
• Get enough sleep so that I am physically energized the next day.

And then I took the following actions:

• Reduced my consumption of fatty foods by 25 percent;
• Created a 30-minute quiet time daily by shutting my office door, forwarding my phone calls, and listening to classical music;
• Changed my habits so that I get seven hours of sleep a night.

Conscious steps to articulate what you value, what you will do to make the value come alive, and what you did to act on the value are crucial in moving from the soft sand of good intentions to the solid ground of strength in the middle of the storm. As Gene Carter began his tenure as Executive Director of ASCD, he held a strong value about cross-functional teaming. When the opportunity arose to build a new ASCD headquarters, Carter seized the opportunity to promote the idea of designing the building infrastructure to promote the core value of cross-functional teaming. "This was a blatant example of acting on our core values. We engaged the entire staff in developing a set of principles and criteria that were going to be embodied in the structure, so that the building became *ours*—not mine, not the board's, not the association's, but ours."

Step 4: Align What You Say, Do, and Value

Action consistent with your values is important, but even more important than action to long-term resilience is aligning the three sets of dynamics shown in the Personal Strengths Triangle (Figure 5.1):

- What you say you value in relation to what you actually value (Say ↔ Value);
- What you say you do in relation to what you actually do (Say ↔ Do);
- What you actually do in relation to what you actually value (Do ↔ Value).

The three anchor points of the Personal Strengths Triangle are Value, Say, and Do. As emphasized previously, *Value* refers to what you believe is important, *Say* refers to what you talk about being important, and *Do* refers to your actions connected to what you say is important. The relationship between what you say you value and what you actually value is a measure of your *authenticity*. Do you, on an ongoing basis, stand up for the values that you say are most important? The relationship

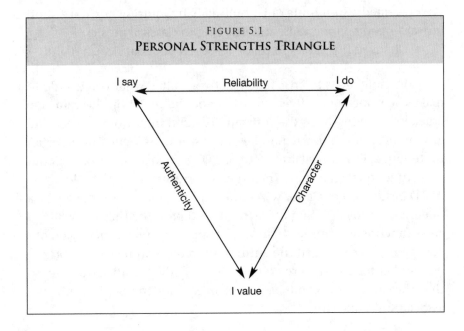

FIGURE 5.1
PERSONAL STRENGTHS TRIANGLE

I say   Reliability   I do

Authenticity

Character

I value

between what you say you do and what you actually do is a measure of your *reliability*. Can you be counted on to follow through consistently in a dependable way by delivering on your commitments to action? The relationship between what you actually do and what you actually value is a measure of your *character*. How do you choose to live your life? Among the three sets of dynamics, the *Do ↔ Value* is the most critical in determining your resilience strength. We have underscored the point that resilience is a long-term concept, not a short-term event. What a person truly values is manifest in what he or she does over the long haul. Your patterns of actions, over an extended period, become outward symbols of your inner character.

The Personal Strengths Triangle is a mirror, reflecting to others who you are. Let's look at how the triangle applies in the following scenario.

Wilson Manning is the newly appointed principal of Westside Elementary, an urban school in the Northeast. He was hired to lead the school in efforts to raise the achievement scores of minority students in the school. Manning is a veteran administrator with more than 30 years in the district, and he has been a longtime, outspoken champion of improving minority performance. In fact, in his most recent principal assignment, his school saw minority achievement on state tests rise 37 percent over a six-year period. It took Manning and his staff a long time, with numerous setbacks along the way. But they did it.

Shortly after Manning accepted the new assignment at Westside, the state legislature passed a law creating incentives for early retirement. Manning was directly affected. He calculated that he could retire at the end of the school year with maximum benefits. With both of his children and his five grandchildren now living on the West Coast, the new retirement incentive became a dominant value to him.

He began the first faculty meeting of the school year with the anticipated refrain, "I am passionate about doing whatever it takes to demonstrate that *all* students in this school learn at high performance levels." Manning's follow-up actions, however, did not match his pronouncements. He invested most of his time in planning for retirement and spent minimal time devoted to improving test scores for minority students.

In this scenario, Principal Manning came to the role at Westside Elementary with the capacity to make a difference in student achievement as he had done in another setting. This time, though, his capacity didn't convert to a strength. Manning didn't have the will to stay the course for the necessary length of time to achieve the goal. And he didn't take the actions to put in motion needed structural changes, such as frequent monitoring of student performance, that he had implemented successfully in the past. Without capacity plus will plus action, potential strength is not realized.

This breakdown shows up as misalignment among the three sets of dynamics:

- *Say ↔ Value:* What Principal Manning said was most important to him was improved minority student performance. What actually mattered most, however, was preparing himself for retirement. In other words, there was a discrepancy between what he said he valued and what he actually valued.
- *Say ↔ Do:* Manning said he would do whatever it took to achieve the goal of improved minority performance. What he actually did was shift his energy to planning for retirement. Misalignment thus occurred between what he said would happen and what actually happened.
- *Do ↔ Value:* Manning could relentlessly insist that his primary value was to improve student achievement. But if his pattern of actions over the course of a year didn't align with his statements about what he values, then the faculty would have to conclude that his repeated choice of actions reflects what he truly values, irrespective of what he said. Such a conclusion would not mean that Principal Manning is a bad person or doesn't care about students. As we discussed earlier in the chapter, there are times when each of us is faced with competing values, and we have to make trade-off choices about how we spend our precious resilience currency. What we do in the form of our actions reflects our decisions, conscious or subconscious, about the hierarchy of our values.

Jim Loehr described during our interview how he works with clients to emphasize and then implement alignment between values and actions. "A value without any concrete, tangible energy investment is really empty," he said. "I ask leaders how they can live their values more fully and how they can translate these values into habitual practices that are real every single day in their culture. Then I discuss the need to become fully engaged as an organization, crafting ways of operating that actually bring you closer in alignment with the vision of the company and your own values as a leader. What can you do as a leadership team that could develop actions that embed these values into the DNA of the company?"

Checking for Alignment

You can make tremendous strides in embedding your values into your own DNA if you periodically check for misalignment among the three sets of dynamics outlined here. Many times a misalignment between your values and actions can be traced to what we call *behavioral drift.* That is, it is natural for you to develop patterns of behavior that have a tendency to drift away from what you truly care about. Particularly in times of adversity, you are under pressure to deliver on a number of fronts, and your values, efficacy, and energy are tested by the pressure. For example, you may spend more time at the office than you intended and skip lunch to meet all of the demands on your schedule.

It's unfair to characterize temporary behavioral drift as a sign of weakness or as a departure from stated values. To help avoid any long-term patterns of behavioral drift, you can develop your own personal "virus shield" to detect misalignment between the three sets of dynamics in the Personal Strengths Triangle. For instance, issue a standing invitation to colleagues and family members to regularly provide candid comments about whether you are "walking your talk." Issue a standing invitation for people to let you know when drift happens. As a leader, you show a sign of strength, not weakness, when you acknowledge that sometimes you will make mistakes and engage in conduct that you didn't intend. By asking for immediate, direct feedback when drift occurs and then taking the necessary steps to bring actions, words, and values into better alignment, you become stronger, ready to tackle bigger battles in the future.

Alicia Thomas, associate superintendent in the North East School District in San Antonio, Texas, emphasized in our interview that feedback is extremely important to her. "I get lots of feedback, and it is really helpful to me, particularly negative feedback. Don't get me wrong," she added. "I don't like to hear it, but at the same time I don't shy away from it. I take the feedback and try to go in the direction that I need to move."

Thomas cited an example of how she invited feedback about meeting with the leadership team and, based on the feedback, reconceptualized how she interacted with the principals and the rest of the leadership team. "I would never have gone there without the feedback," she said. "But we are fundamentally changing how we do business together next year. I am really excited about it."

Another way to check consistently for alignment among your values, words, and actions is to use a format similar to that presented in the Checking for Alignment Inventory shown in Figure 5.2. You can apply this format to any core value. In completing the inventory, you may follow these simple guidelines:

1. Develop your core value and *I will* statements, and place them in the "Key Point" column.

2. Assign a point value (1–5) to how important each key point is to you. Typically, because you have declared each of these items a *key* point, their importance value will be high, a 5 or 4.

3. Check for alignment by asking others to indicate the extent to which your intentions are being effectively met, as measured by your pattern of behavior.

FIGURE 5.2
CHECKING FOR ALIGNMENT INVENTORY

Key Point	Importance	Effectiveness	Gap
Value: I value making a difference in the lives of students	5	4	1
I will • Organize my time so that I focus first on students' needs	5	5	0
• Create forums so I can listen carefully to students talking about their needs	5	2	3
• Make sure that my career path keeps me in a role that serves students	5	3	2

4. Conduct a gap analysis to identify areas for follow-up action. When you analyze the data, look for the areas with the greatest discrepancy between importance and effectiveness.

5. Use data from the gap analysis as a basis for action. By constructing a framework that includes task, time line, resources needed, and indicators of accomplishment, you can build an action plan that brings your intentions and your actions into closer alignment.

By periodically checking for alignment, you can detect patterns of drift before they become entrenched negative habits that are harder to correct. Also, by taking early action on the behavioral drift, you spend your resilience currency on building a strength rather than fighting a large, accumulated deficit between intentions and actual conduct.

The Anguish of Acting on Your Convictions

What we have described in the chapter so far represents a *rational* conceptual framework for constructing and acting on core values. We are under no illusion, however, that the real world of leading occurs in a rational environment. In fact, as Patterson (2003) argues, school leaders try to stay true to their convictions in the midst of "nonrational organizations" characterized by multiple and competing goals, power struggles among competing forces, decision-making processes influenced by politics and deal making, and an external environment that imposes self-serving agendas on the organization. Add to this the ingredient of scarce resources, and school leaders may find it extremely difficult to stay the course of acting in alignment with their values.

During our interview, Paul Houston commented, "When it comes to acting on the courage of your convictions, I would argue that those who don't act don't have the convictions. They have assertions. There is a difference. We can all assert stuff. For instance, I believe all kids can learn. For most people, that is just an assertion, because they don't act on it."

Houston also suggested that many people have too many core values. "Part of convictions is having so few of them that you can act on them," he said. "There is probably a workable limit to what you feel about strongly enough so you can take action. If you had convictions on a hundred things, to be extreme, you would probably render yourself incapable of acting on anything. . . . You have to choose which ones are the most important to make a difference for you and the people you are working with. Those are the ones you make your stands on."

Many interviewees reinforced Houston's contention and spoke candidly about both the anguish and the courage of taking tough stands. Here we discuss three sets of pressure conditions that complicate a school leader's ability to act in accordance with her values: taking urgent action in the thick of the storm, taking action contrary to the advice by colleagues you trust, and taking action in the face of stormy opposition.

Taking Urgent Action

Sometimes anguish stems from the pressure to make quick, urgent decisions in line with your convictions. Carol Choye, superintendent of schools in the Scotch Plains–Fanwood, New Jersey, School District, described one situation that she faced.

"We had a 7th grade girl in the office threatening to commit suicide. Her parents were there but didn't have a car to take her to the hospital. The parents were pacing and crying. The girl was crying. The mother said she would wait and take her to the hospital the next day. I felt this was an urgent situation, so I decided to take the girl in the car myself. Someone said, 'You can't do that,' and I responded, 'Watch me.' I got a hastily signed permission form and took the girl to the psychiatric unit of the hospital. The staff in the unit said, 'We have never had a superintendent come here before with a student.' Later I took the family out for dinner. When I returned to school the next day, people said, 'That is just incredible what you did.' I couldn't figure out why everyone was so surprised." From Choye's perspective, her quick actions were driven by her convictions, and she felt it was just the "natural" thing to do.

A less traumatic but still pivotal pressure point faced Rubén Olivárez at his first board meeting. During a presentation by the administration, the board of education started interrogating one of Olivárez's staff members, sending a clear message about who was in control. Olivárez sized up the situation and took quick action.

"I asked the staff member to sit down, and I took her place at the podium, facing the board," he told us. "Then I asked them what they needed to know. A board member replied that I didn't have the information. And I said rather emphatically that I was the superintendent and would get the information if I didn't have it directly. The board president decided to move on to the next agenda item. I stayed standing at the podium. The board president then seemed a bit uncomfortable and asked me to join them again at the table. I said if they were going to interrogate other staff members that way, I would just stay where I was. The president said, rather humbly, to please come back to the table to join them."

Olivárez told us that this was a defining moment in his relationship with the board, and his strong stance represented a major risk for him as a rookie superintendent. When we asked Olivárez why he took such action with so much at stake, he shrugged his shoulders and said matter-of-factly, "I did it because it was the right thing to do at the moment. It all goes back to my belief system [core values]."

Taking Action Contrary to Advice

At times the anguish of actions is precipitated by school leaders acting in opposition to advice by supervisors and peers. Linda Hanson faced this situation as a high school principal.

"Some high school students walked out of the school in protest over an issue," she explained. "Not only did they walk out, but they had coordinated it with two middle schools. It occurred over the lunch hour, so many other students who did not participate in the walkout were out of the building, too. My supervisor, the assistant superintendent, called and told us to lock the kids out and not let them back in. I said, 'No, I'm not going to do that.' He said, 'Well, why wouldn't you do it? I'm telling you to.' I said, 'Well, first of all, I would be locking out kids who legitimately didn't walk out. Second, I don't think it's safe to lock kids out. We don't know which situations they have for riding home. It's Illinois, it's cold, and I just don't think it's safe.' He said, 'Well, I'm telling you I want the kids locked out.' I said, 'I'm telling you, I'm not going to do it.' He said, 'Then let me tell you, downtown [the central office] is telling you to lock the kids out.' And I said, 'Then you tell downtown to come here and lock them out,' and I hung up."

As Hanson reflected on the ordeal, she commented, "Part of my learning in that was if you are going to take a lot of criticism, it might as well be on what you believe, and not what someone else believes."

Carter faced opposition in his first year as superintendent in Norfolk. "The first year of my superintendency in Norfolk was a year the school district struggled with the busing issue and returning to neighborhood schools. There was a segment of the black community who said their kids couldn't get the education they needed in the neighborhood. And some black board members opposed the move to neighborhood schools. And it fell upon me as the first black superintendent of the city to come to grips with the issue and provide leadership to restructure the school district to fit the decision we made. So that year was a tough year.

"That was a threshold moment for me," Carter added. "All of the senior administrators were white except for one black assistant superintendent. The one black assistant superintendent was vehemently against what I was supporting. It was a challenge to get the team together, the board together, and a splintered community together."

In the face of the adversity and strong opposition, Carter moved ahead with actions consistent with his strong convictions about what was in the best interests of the students and the larger community. In his view, the outcome was worth the price paid.

Taking Action in the Face of Opposition

Sometimes the opposition is much more fierce than colleagues holding diverse perspectives. In Chapter 3, we recounted how Vince Ferrandino took strong action in the face of threats to him and his family. Houston discussed a similar set of circumstances facing his colleague and mentor, Neil Sullivan, who was asked by President John Kennedy to open a school district that had been shut down for having segregated schools. According to Houston, "Neil Sullivan was a man who had a deep abiding conviction about minority kids having a fair chance in life, and his own life was built around that. So he went down to this rural school district in Virginia, opened the school district, and the repercussions were incredible. They bombed his house, shot through his windows, but do you know what? Sullivan didn't flinch. He was so sure that what he was doing was so important and needed to be done that he considered all of these terrible things to be mere nuisances that he had to endure to get the job done."

Houston then said that he can recall hundreds of superintendents who lost their jobs because they stood up for their convictions. This moral courage doesn't make them heroes. Several leaders whom we interviewed said that there were times they stood up for their convictions, only to reflect later that they were wrong. But they repeatedly said that they didn't judge themselves by their inevitable, individual mistakes along the way. They judged themselves by the patterns of their conduct over time consistent with their values.

Many times the courage comes from reflecting on past performance and realizing misalignment between values and actions. Gerrita Postlewait said that earlier in her career, she didn't always find the courage to be honest with people about her frustrations with them. Then she learned a lesson about courage in one of the most popular classrooms for school leaders, the parking lot.

"One day in the parking lot, I saw a friend who said she was getting company, and I commented that it seemed like it was always so much work to get ready. And she said, 'No, it isn't. I love my family too much to feel frustrated about everything I have to prepare and then annoyed that I have to clean up after them. So I just tell them to come cooking and leave cleaning.' "

Back in her car, Postlewait realized that this good advice applied to herself at work. She started to act in concert with her convictions in the area of honest dialogue. She conveyed the message "I care about you too much to feel inconvenienced by the bickering that goes on. I just need to tell you how it makes me feel and how it gets in the way from our being able to work together." Postlewait observed, "Once I came back and put this idea in practice, a whole new world opened up. People appreciated my being honest with them."

Ben Canada summarized the importance of acting on convictions this way: "I've got a quote on the wall that guides me. It says, 'Watch your thoughts for they become your words. Watch your words for they become actions. Watch your actions because they become habits. Watch your habits for they become character. Watch your character for it becomes your destiny.' I try to live by that. For me, the courage to live up to my convictions is the inner strength that allows me to be who I am."

It also allows you to be more resilient after the storm.

6

PERSONAL EFFICACY

Our desire to control our environment, to exercise personal agency, is as old as humankind. Over the centuries, philosophers and theologians have debated our desires for dominion and the extent of human capability through discussions of free will and determinism. In the last 30 years, current understanding of personal efficacy as a psychological concept evolved from social cognitive theory. Among its principles is the assumption that your sense of self and the social contexts in which you live and work have reciprocal influences. The context in which you live and work influences who you are, including self-efficacy beliefs, and who you are influences the environment in which you live and work. From this perspective, you do not just believe what you see; you also see what you believe (Maddux, 2002). This chapter will discuss the power of personal efficacy to affect what you see and, therefore, what you believe. We will first define what research tells us efficacy is and then discuss why it is important.

What Efficacy Is and Is Not

Personal efficacy refers to your beliefs about your capability to accomplish challenging goals. Psychological research suggests that you think of your self-efficacy beliefs as a filter through which you evaluate your past experiences and make judgments about what you choose to try to accomplish in the future. As a filter for your experience, self-efficacy beliefs define the strength of your sense of personal mastery, your confidence in your abilities to make an impact.

Psychological research also offers powerful evidence that the level and strength of your self-efficacy affects the quality and success of your performance (Bandura, 1997, p. 72). For example, an elementary principal—let's call her Betsy Grundy—has achieved extraordinary success in a school in which she hired most of the teachers, developed relationships with them over a period of years, built the academic program, and nurtured strong relationships with students' parents and the community. Because of her success in improving student achievement, her superintendent has persuaded her to accept a transfer to a low-performing school. In her new environment, her first change initiatives meet stiff faculty and parent resistance. She suddenly feels ineffective and, in fact, does not seem like the same educational leader—not as confident, not as competent. What happened? In her new school, her self-efficacy beliefs have taken a nosedive, in part because the results she has come to expect from her work no longer seem to her to be achievable. Her weakened self-efficacy has led to lower-quality performance, in her judgment and in that of her superintendent.

It is possible, even likely, that as Grundy's new environment becomes more familiar, as she develops new networks of people on whom she can rely, that her self-efficacy will rebound and she will be successful again. But psychological research suggests that it is also possible that if Grundy does not regain her belief that she is capable as the principal of orchestrating high-level success for the teachers and students in her new school, she will not be as successful there as she was in her previous school. The level and strength of your self-efficacy beliefs are indeed strong predictors of the results that you achieve. Your beliefs about what you can accomplish determine what you choose to do in face of adversity and how long and much you persevere in the face of obstacles (Maddux, 2002, p. 285).

In her new school, away from a social context that supported her self-efficacy beliefs, Grundy no longer feels as capable. Her self-doubt means that she does not "see," or credit herself for, the small successes (e.g., the veteran teacher who is grateful for her curriculum suggestion), which are probably the best she can hope for in the early days in her new environment as she tries to build trusting relationships with strangers.

In describing the power of personal efficacy and the impact when it is weakened, we are not suggesting that you can control your life totally through your beliefs. A number of forces besides your individual will and action help determine the course that your life takes, including social, geographic, and institutional influences. For example, no matter how strongly Principal Grundy believes in her ability to inspire faculty growth and improvement, her teachers may not be as capable as her previous faculty in strengthening student achievement. Nevertheless, you can improve your life and take charge of your future to the extent that you do control events. And you may discover that you have more control over the outcome of events than you initially thought. If Grundy recovers her belief in her ability to lead the faculty to change, they are more apt to reach their potential, whatever its level, than if her self-doubt takes permanent root.

As the variability in our fictional principal's confidence in her capability suggests, efficacy is not fixed. It is not a personality trait engrained from childhood. It is a self-assurance that develops through successful mastery experiences. But it cannot necessarily be generalized or transferred. You may hold strong self-efficacy beliefs in one area of your work or life and weaker ones in another. And, as Grundy's story illustrates, self-efficacy is highly contextual. The development of efficacy, then, is a dynamic process, the result of interaction between the self and the environment. In general, your efficacy grows stronger as a result of successful coping with adversity, with life's storms.

Grundy's case also illustrates another important distinction. Self-efficacy is a *belief* as distinguished from a skill, an action, and even an intention to act (Maddux, 2002, p. 278). In her new school, Grundy's repertoire of skills has not deteriorated. It's her self-confidence that has been undermined.

A nonresponsive environment does not always lead to self-doubt or lower personal efficacy. On the contrary, you can maintain strong efficacy beliefs in either a responsive or a nonresponsive environment. Where strong efficacy beliefs are coupled with a responsive environment, and your expectations about outcomes are high, "productive engagement, aspiration, and personal satisfaction" characterize your behavior and attitude (see Figure 6.1). Where strong efficacy is coupled with a nonresponsive environment, you tend to respond with "protest, grievance, social activism, or milieu change" (Bandura, 1995, p. 20).

Weak efficacy beliefs combined with a nonresponsive environment and low outcome expectations suggest that you may respond with "resignation and apathy." These burnout consequences are the greatest danger for Principal Grundy.

As Grundy struggles with these issues, it may be helpful for her to distinguish efficacy beliefs—the "I can"—from locus-of-control beliefs—the "I may not be able to because of circumstances beyond my control."

FIGURE 6.1
EFFICACY–ENVIRONMENT INTERACTION

	Responsive Environment	Nonresponsive Environment
Strong Efficacy	Productive engagement, aspiration, and personal satisfaction	Protest, grievance, social activism, or "milieu change"
Weak Efficacy	Devaluation, despondency	Resignation, apathy, burnout

Source: Adapted from *Self-Efficacy: The Exercise of Control,* p. 20, by A. Bandura, 1997, New York: W. H. Freeman.

Perceived personal efficacy beliefs and locus of control bear little or no relationship (Bandura, 1995, p. 20). That is, you can maintain healthy self-confidence in your ability to get the job done but recognize that you still may not have enough control of other factors to be successful. Your options, then, are to protest or challenge your lack of power in some way or to find another job. As we will describe later, school leaders tend to have strong efficacy beliefs. At the same time, they express frustration, disappointment, and anger because they often do not have sufficient control to achieve the level of success of which they feel capable.

Personal efficacy is a powerful personal attribute. In fact, as a filter for all your experience, self-efficacy is so powerful that psychologists now believe that all "processes of psychological and behavioral change operate through the alteration" of your sense of personal mastery (Maddux, 1995, p. 7). From this perspective, your efficacy beliefs generate the energy and motivation that lead you to set goals, to choose actions to achieve those goals, to invest effort in those actions, and to persevere in the face of obstacles. Efficacy also affects the feelings you have along the way—for example, satisfaction if you are achieving success and disappointment if you are struggling. Finally, efficacy leads to taking advantage of opportunities that present themselves unexpectedly in an organizational setting and also to circumventing institutional constraints and galvanizing people for collective action (Bandura, 1995, p. 6).

In summary, personal efficacy refers to your beliefs about your capability to accomplish challenging goals. It does not refer to the skills you possess, the goals you actually set, or the actions you choose to undertake in pursuit of those goals. Personal efficacy, however, influences all of these. In fact, psychological research suggests that your ability to enact changes in yourself and the environment depends on altering your beliefs about your personal mastery first. Personal efficacy varies with the kind of challenge you face and its context. Finally, success in weathering a life storm generally strengthens personal efficacy.

Why Self-Efficacy Is Important

A growing body of evidence indicates that "optimistic self-efficacy" is essential to human accomplishment and positive well-being (Bandura, 1995, p. 72). The stronger your self-efficacy beliefs, the more challenging the goals that you embrace, and the greater your achievements. As we have said, the strength of your beliefs affects how strong your commitments are, determines what you choose to do in the face of adversity, and influences how long you persevere in the effort despite obstacles (Maddux, 2002, p. 282).

Personal efficacy enables you to influence events that otherwise might seem beyond your control. Educators often enter the profession feeling a "calling," a moral mission to improve the lives of children. You desire to shape the future. Though efficacy is not the sole determinant of your actions, it is highly correlated with your ability to affect the complex environment that you work in and that often seems intractable to your influence. Optimistic self-efficacy contributes to your sense of personal agency in these challenging moments (Bandura, 1995, p. 75).

Shaping the future means changing the present. As you know, change threatens conventional views, and proposals to make significant changes predictably meet with resistance and even rejection. History is replete with stories of the obstacles that innovators have met and had to overcome. When Robert Goddard first proposed rocket propulsion, for example, his scientific colleagues soundly rejected his ideas as unworkable. Great artists, such as the first Impressionist painters who could not for many years get their paintings shown in the annual Paris Salon, may experience years of rejection by contemporary critics. In fact, rejection of innovation is so predictable that it has become cliché. The story of the unappreciated, creative genius who spends a lifetime in poverty, enduring social isolation and even ostracism, is familiar to all of us.

An unshakable sense of personal efficacy is what enables people who have shaped the future of their fields to bear the criticism and rejection and to persevere in spite of little or no obvious chance of immediate success (Robert White as cited in Bandura, 1995, p. 72). In fact, research suggests that the personal efficacy of these achievers is itself "optimistic." Those who are successful in achieving challenging goals tend to have an exaggerated estimation of their own capabilities. Optimists sometimes aim a little too high in their goals but, in the process, achieve more than they would if their goals were less ambitious. "One does not find many pragmatic realists in the ranks of innovators and greater achievers" (Bandura, 1995, p. 74). And the optimistic view of their own self-efficacy sustains their motivation and persistence through the tough times. You do not want to tilt at windmills. But if you lack confidence, you will tend to be conservative in your willingness to act and to take risks. And it is difficult at best to assess the cost of lost opportunities and the lack of development of potential capability, the "cost of promising courses of action not taken" (Bandura, 1995, p. 71).

Several of the school leaders whom we interviewed for this volume manifest optimistic self-efficacy. They described, for example, daunting situations, often in public board meetings, where they reached inside themselves and found a verbal response to a challenge that carried the day in spite of long odds. They took a risk, and it paid off. Often, they would say in retrospect, "I don't know where it came from, how I thought of it, but it worked."

Philosophers and psychologists both suggest that the importance of personal efficacy lies not only in your achievements but also in your happiness. A sense of control over your environment, behavior, and thoughts is essential to feelings of well-being. Low self-efficacy correlates with a number of psychological problems, including depression and dysfunctional anxiety. Depressed people have less confidence in their abilities than others, even though they may have the same actual level of skills. They have a more realistic estimate of their self-efficacy than the optimists just described, but they accomplish less because they aim lower in setting goals and give up sooner (Bandura, 1995, p. 74). Those who experience high levels of anxiety often begin efforts with lower self-efficacy than others. In a downward spiral, their anxiety can then "disrupt performance" (Maddux, 2002, p. 281), lowering self-efficacy even further.

Enhancing personal efficacy is essential to adopting and maintaining "virtually every behavior" (Maddux, 2002, p. 281) that produces physical health, including diet and exercise, stress management, smoking cessation, and alcohol use and abuse. Self-efficacy affects physiological responses that, in turn, affect physical health, such as stress responses, immune system responses, and susceptibility to infection (Maddux, 2002, p. 281).

Because of these psychological and physiological impacts of low-ered self-efficacy, we have cause to worry about the principal in our narrative, Betsy Grundy, as she labors in this transition period between success in her old school and hoped-for success in her new one. Because the evidence of the connections between efficacy and health and happiness are so strong, she will have to be alert to these negative effects. Grundy has always had good health. In the past, she has bene-fited from the positive life-enhancing psychological and physiological effects of a strong sense of efficacy. In her new school, she will have to be especially careful about tending to her physical health and taking care of herself—eating well, sleeping enough, and attending her regular fitness classes with her close friends.

Loehr and Schwartz (2003) describe another danger that can result from low self-efficacy. In these circumstances, in which Grundy knows that she is not as effective as she was in her previous school, the stress of work may become addictive. "Stress hormones such as adrenaline, noradrenaline, and cortisol fuel arousal and create a seductive rush—the so-called adrenaline high" (p. 39).

As with many educators, Grundy has a highly, perhaps overly, devel-oped sense of responsibility. She has a strong sense of personal mission: to provide the best learning environment possible for the children in her charge. Because she is so hard on herself, she is particularly prone to deny herself respites for energy renewal and recovering. She is suscepti-ble, then, to stress addiction—working chronically long hours, becom-ing overextended, being sleep deprived, and running on empty. Nothing will deplete her efficacy reserves faster or more completely than stress addiction.

In conclusion, strong personal efficacy enables you to attempt more challenging goals, "see" greater success, and, therefore, believe in your greater capability. Efficacy and achievement have mutually rein-forcing influences on each other, increasing your sense of personal agency. Stronger personal efficacy correlates with your positive physi-cal and psychological consequences—good health and happiness. In the next chapter, you will see how school leaders translate these research-based theories about personal efficacy into action.

7

How Leaders Sustain
and Strengthen
Personal Efficacy

In this chapter, we will look at efficacy in action—how school leaders both sustain and strengthen their personal efficacy capacity. We identify crucial building blocks of efficacy: confidence and competence, as well as strong connections to others. We also describe strategies that successful school leaders employ to strengthen these qualities.

Confidence and Competence

Your confidence and competence are key indicators of your personal efficacy, and confidence and competence are inextricably connected. Increased self-confidence leads to undertaking more challenging tasks and to developing higher levels of competence. Greater competence in turn increases self-confidence in a positive, upward spiral. Successful school leaders use several strategies to strengthen confidence and competence.

Build a Sense of Mastery

When you are young and inexperienced, you may tend to devalue experience. Through the filter of your youthful, often-untried efficacy beliefs, you see some older people simply repeating the same experience over and over again without seeming to learn or grow from it. And you may legitimately argue that this kind of experience has little value. As you grow older, you realize that successful experience expands your knowledge and increases your skills. In other words, it builds your competence and strengthens your self-confidence.

Successful experience that positively affects personal efficacy, though, does involve developing "self-regulatory tools" that enable you to undertake effective actions in the face of changing circumstances (Bandura, 1995, p. 80). Among those tools is *self-reflection,* the ability to analyze and appraise your experience and to learn from it. Many other factors besides self-evaluation of your performance, of course, influence how your success or failure will affect your efficacy beliefs—among them your preconceptions about your abilities, the difficulty of the challenges that you have undertaken, and other external circumstances. Nevertheless, self-reflection about your experience can strengthen your competence and confidence.

In chapter 3, Linda Hanson told about how as a young administrator she did not feel firmly "grounded" in her own philosophy about teaching and learning. She recalled having a leadership role in a process to "totally change the direction of instruction" and remembered a "sick feeling in her stomach" as she asked herself, "Am I doing the best thing for kids?" In retrospect, she thought that the changes that she and her teachers had made were, in fact, valuable. This experience strengthened her efficacy. And she credited her self-reflection for helping her persevere despite her self-doubts: "Probably the single thing I have done the most as an instructional leader is to have used myself as a laboratory— when I say, 'Well, how do I learn that? Under what circumstances . . . would this work for me or wouldn't it work? Would it work for my kids?' And so often that clarifies." Using herself as a "laboratory" was a key self-regulatory tool through which Hanson filtered her experience and made judgments about future actions. Her success in this cycle of self-reflection and action enabled her to develop "faith in herself and the tenacity"—self-efficacy—to continue to undertake and persevere in difficult and complex tasks.

For mastery experiences to affect efficacy positively, they need to be challenging. If you only have easy successes, then you expect quick results and don't learn how to deal with adversity and failure. "A resilient sense of efficacy requires experience in overcoming obstacles through perseverant effort" (Bandura, 1995, p. 80).

As with all successful school leaders, Hanson took on challenging goals that presented obstacles, tested her, and strengthened her tenacity. She described one of these initiatives: "I had two high schools, and they were both very suspicious of each other. . . . So I decided to start the Leadership Academy. The Leadership Academy is where one administrator would go to the opposite school . . . and switch places for a year.

And I . . . mandated that they had to do it. There were some real unhappy people in the beginning. And that took tenacity to see it through because . . . they were grumbly.

"It turned out to be wonderful. It turned out to be a great, great thing. And actually it turned out to be great for the individuals who partook of it because three of them went out after that experience and became principals in other places because they had just enough of a step up. That was a place where I really needed tenacity."

As an experienced superintendent in Sarasota, Florida, Chuck Fowler had developed a strong sense of personal mastery and concomitant strong sense of self-efficacy. These qualities fueled his commitment and tenacity to take on significant challenges that further confirmed the success of his values-based leadership.

"When I went there in 1985," Fowler told us, "in that county and in most of Florida, corporal punishment was still permitted. It wasn't widely practiced in our school district, but it was there, and I knew psychologically and educationally this was a poor policy. But there were other people who were of the 'If it's not broke, don't fix it' mentality. And I think in 1986 the legislature made it optional. . . . So we became the first county in Florida that acted on that authority, and we just abolished it.

"Again people would say, 'Don't go there—kids aren't really being hurt by this, and it's not a big enough issue for you to stake your professional life on this issue.' But I felt so strongly that it was wrong, even if there were only one victim of it. And I knew that with proper education, the board would agree with me and set the policy. It became like a domino effect. We adopted it one month. Another county adopted it three months later, and within a matter of a couple of years, probably . . . two-thirds of the counties ruled [corporal punishment] out.

"For me it was an adaptive issue," Fowler remarked. "You could look at it technically and justify abolishing it just on technical grounds because it creates too great a liability, personal injury risk, that sort of thing. But it was just not right. That was enough to drive me to try to get that accomplished."

Set Short-Term Goals and Benchmarks of Progress

Another key strategy that successful school leaders use to strengthen confidence and competence is to set and achieve specific, attainable and assessable goals. Actively envisioning some concrete short-term and desired outcome—as opposed to only articulating an abstract, indeterminate, remote goal—can motivate you, shape your actions, define your competence, and ultimately provide real evidence of efficacy. Indefinite goals do not help you decide which activities to choose or how much effort to invest. Indefinite goals also give you no useful information for evaluating your performance. You cannot unambiguously know that you have successfully gotten somewhere unless you know in advance where you are trying to go. You cannot be fully satisfied and feel competent about what you have done unless your accomplishment clearly fulfills personal goals that you have set (Maddux, 2002, p. 283).

An example of the motivational power of specific, short-term goals comes from marathon running. As an endurance runner you learn early not to define the goal as completing 26 miles in a certain time. You must break the whole into parts in order not to become overwhelmed, intimidated, and defeated by the pain that running 26 miles entails. A first goal may be to run the first five miles in a certain time and then see how you feel. At that point, you can experience early success in meeting your first target and set a second goal—the next five miles—and adjust the hoped-for time according to your performance so far.

The scholars and practitioners whom we interviewed for this volume certainly confirmed the value of setting focused, short-terms goals. Tom Sergiovanni, for example, stated, "I think there are two virtues that have to do with whatever success I've had, and neither of them has to do with what you know or how smart you are. One is . . . to be able to have a razor-sharp focus on a handful of things that are really important to you. [The other is to] try not to dilute what you're doing at first across the whole spectrum of the rainbow, so to speak." As Sergiovanni suggested, short-term, attainable, specific goals not only provide a "razor-sharp focus" for energies and actions but also help you avoid distractions that can dilute efforts, attenuate success, and lead to lower self-efficacy.

Carol Choye confirmed in practice short-term goals' value to success. She became involved in a strategic planning process that laid out a global vision of school district aspirations but failed to provide the impetus and motivation necessary to galvanize people's attention and energies. "You had hundreds of people involved with strategic planning," she said. "But one of the things you didn't have was community and staff action planning. . . . A very supportive board . . . said it's not enough just to have a strategic plan; you need to come to us and tell us on a year-to-year basis what the priorities are. We . . . developed a model so that every year we could fine-tune." "Chunking out" the strategic plan into smaller annual goals helped Choye mobilize resources and achieve greater competence.

Interestingly, though, research suggests that accomplishment of a challenging goal does not automatically lead to strengthened competence, confidence, and the desire to achieve even more challenging goals. Unlike Choye and Fowler, some people feel enough self-doubt, even after a success that came with difficulty, that they do not want to invest themselves so totally again. Some judge that the cost of success was too high and choose not to set such challenging goals again. Some of the school leaders whom we interviewed evinced this attitude. They felt good about what they had accomplished—for example, in convincing a reluctant community to support a reorganization of grade-level structure that meant some families would attend different schools—and experienced no loss of self-efficacy. However, they felt, overall, that the cost to them personally was too great in terms of time invested, hostility faced, and pain felt.

Claim Small Wins

As a professional educator like Betsy Grundy, the principal whom we introduced in the previous chapter, you probably have high expectations for yourself. If, like her, you also have an overdeveloped sense of responsibility, when things go wrong, you may see yourself as deficient in knowledge and skills. Plagued with self-doubts, you may be unable to see and take credit for small successes, even when those around you try to point them out. This negative cycle spirals downward. Lower personal efficacy means less ability to see success and to achieve competence, which means less confidence and even lower self-efficacy.

If you can learn to claim your successes, however, you can avoid or reverse the cycle. Your efficacy will spiral upward if you, first, view your competencies not as immutable, God-given traits but as abilities that you acquire through experience and effort and apply incrementally in particular contexts (Maddux, 2002, p. 284). If Grundy can remember that she acquired her skills over time and through hard work in her previous job and that she achieved success with them slowly and incrementally, she may be better able to see and take credit for her small wins in her new school, as she continues to develop skills and builds success one person and one situation at a time.

You can reverse the negative personal efficacy spiral, second, by retraining your attribution reflexes. People who attribute success to their personal skills and failure to lack of effort will undertake more difficult tasks and persevere in them for longer than those who reflexively attribute success to situational factors and failure to their own lack of skill (Bandura, 1995, pp. 122–123). If you believe in the power of effort, then, when you hit obstacles, you will be motivated to work harder in applying your skills. As a result, you may achieve more success and higher levels of competence as well as feel more confident about your skills. If Grundy can begin to see her small successes (e.g., each time she helps one teacher strengthen a lesson or solve a student problem) as a result of her leadership skills rather than give credit only to the teacher or some other factor, she can get back on the attribution road that leads to greater efficacy.

The third way to enhance your ability to claim success and strengthen your efficacy is to allow yourself and those who support you to inflate your estimate of your own capabilities. As discussed earlier, some positive distortion in your self-efficacy can lead you to more efficacy-enhancing success (Maddux, 2002, p. 284). Obviously, if this positive distortion becomes an illusion of grandiosity, it will be destructive. In Grundy's case, however, her superintendent and other supporters would do well to be generous in their feedback about her abilities. If her self-confidence increases, she will accomplish more, be better able to claim her successes, and feel better about herself.

Recover Quickly from Setbacks

Another strategy for strengthening confidence and competence is to recover quickly from setbacks. Effective action requires both competence and the confidence to be successful. Talented people with the skills, like Grundy, can undermine themselves by self-doubt that weakens their efficacy. As we have reiterated, storms happen; adversity sets in. "Self-doubt can set in fast after failures and reversals" (Bandura, 1995, p. 72). The problem is not that adversity produces self-doubt. That's a normal, human reaction. As discussed in Chapter 1, the issue is how quickly you recover your sense of efficacy after these events. Research shows that speed of recovery "separates high achievers from those who settle for lesser accomplishments" (Bandura, 1995, p. 95).

Effective school leaders recognize that the complexity of their jobs means that oversights and other mistakes are inevitable. They have learned to rebound. What's more, they value the personal flexibility that allows them to recover quickly from setbacks. In Chapter 3, we related Ben Canada's story about the state of the district address he delivered. As he publicly declared his plans, he looked over at the board members' faces and realized that he had not informed them in advance of his remarks, so that they could be prepared and not surprised.

Most, if not all, school leaders have found themselves in Canada's situation with one constituency or another. They understand to their core that communication with all interest groups, especially the board, is critical. Nevertheless, in their messy and fragmented work world, they also know that oversights like this one happen. The issue is not that you fail to communicate occasionally. The issue, instead, is how quickly you recover. Here is how Canada recovered: "Well, I think you can be flexible in setting your strategies to recover from setbacks. . . . I immediately went back to the board and acknowledged that I'd made the mistake. And though I believed in what I was doing, my capacity to get it done was greatly diminished without their support of it, and I was now asking for support after the fact. In the future I would make every effort not to put them in that predicament again. And I did get their support."

If Canada had simply ignored the looks that he saw on board members' faces or if his personal efficacy beliefs had been damaged by their nonverbal feedback and he became defensive as a result, then this situation might have quickly have become irrecoverable. Instead, he acted quickly, using his communication skills effectively, and won their support. The combination of his intact efficacy beliefs and his skills allowed a speedy recovery.

Psychological research suggests that, under adversity, many individuals and organizations respond in ways that inhibit their ability to be flexible and to recover quickly (Weick, 2003, p. 75). Rather than trying to get more and better information about the nature of the crisis, under stress they become defensive, narrow their information processing and thus ignore vital data that might help their understanding of the storm that they face and how to respond effectively. In contrast, resilient individuals and organizations, in the face of a storm and despite the stress, respond flexibly. They broaden their information processing, seeking more and better information about the nature of the storm. As noted in Chapter 5, Alicia Thomas told us about hearing negative feedback from both subordinates and her boss—that central office meetings with principals needed to be revamped. Although she initially and reflexively felt the natural tendency to be defensive that most of us would feel in this situation, she learned to respond constructively to criticism. She quickly met with her staff, shared the information, and developed changes that addressed the concerns. As she said, "We're really changing how we do business for next year, totally. But I'm kind of excited about it."

Thomas's openness to negative information means that she will more quickly get better information about impending storms and be better able to forecast consequences and minimize their negative effects. The negative information that she had received about meeting structure allowed her to forecast a storm to her own staff and to make changes that would support quick recovery. As a result of her flexibility, she was able to change "how we do business" (i.e., become more competent) and to feel good about her responsiveness, a positive sense that enhances her confidence.

Manage Yourself

Your physical and emotional states clearly affect and are affected by your sense of confidence and competence. The impact of your physical state occurs, for example, when you associate physiological indicators—such as clammy hands, rapid heart beat, or flushed face—with actual or perceived poor performance. It also occurs, conversely, when you associate other indicators—dry hands, regular heartbeat, and beaming face—with success. A similar impact occurs when you associate certain emotional states—anxiety, alarm—with failure and other states—calmness, content—with success (Maddux, 2002, p. 280).

Because you feel a stronger sense of efficacy when you are calm than when you are upset, strategies for controlling negative feelings, especially anxiety, are crucially important (Maddux, 2002, p. 283). Anxiety not only reduces self-efficacy but also degrades your competence because it disrupts your focus, concentration, and ability to employ your skills as effectively as you can. Managing your emotions to reduce negative, destructive feelings and to strengthen positive efficacy-inducing feelings is a key element of emotional intelligence that we will discuss in more depth in the next chapter.

Some of the school leaders whom we interviewed have consciously developed and implemented self-control strategies to stay calm—and effective—during emotion-fraught meetings. Hanson told us, "You've got a parent who's in your face, and you break eye contact, and you start writing. It gives you another thing to concentrate on; it cools you down." Canada, too, kept his cool at difficult times by writing notes to himself: "I developed a process in taking notes—critical points that somebody was making—and at other times I doodled, and at other times I'd say something comical, make a little comical note to myself about what it is that this person said." In the turmoil of a heated moment, both Canada and Hanson were able to disengage themselves from becoming too emotionally involved by carrying on an internal dialogue through a notepad. As Canada said, "You're having a dialogue with yourself and giving the impression that you're also seriously concerned about what it is that they are saying."

Taking care of physical health as well as emotional health is also essential to sustaining your self-confidence and high levels of competence. Self-efficacy affects biological processes that, in turn, affect your health. Lowered self-efficacy weakens feelings of personal agency and mastery and increases feelings of stress. Stress can have many deleterious effects, including a weaker immune system. When you perceive yourself as lacking control over what happens to you, you are more susceptible to infections and other diseases, and the progress of disease is more apt to accelerate (Bandura, 1997, p. 262).

An enhanced sense of self-efficacy, in contrast, is essential to changing unhealthy behavior and to following through on efforts to improve your health. Strong self-efficacy correlates with every aspect of healthy behavior, including diet, exercise, smoke cessation, safe sex, and avoidance of alcohol abuse (Maddux, 2002, p. 281). Our interviewees were keenly aware of the importance of taking care of physical health and actively committed to healthy behaviors that improve physical fitness. We talk more about specific examples of these behaviors in Chapter 9.

Strong Connections to Others

Personal efficacy, as Betsy Grundy's case demonstrates, is highly contextual. Grundy is not the same principal in her new school as she was in her old one. All of the circumstances of her leadership are different, as are the people around her. Recognizing that variability is a fact of life, you can still improve your chances of maintaining your efficacy at a high level and of performing at or near your peak by staying closely connected to people around you who can provide both professional and personal support to your efforts. The school leaders whom we interviewed described several strategies for maintaining and increasing strong connections to others.

Believe in the Power of the Team

In effective organizations, efficacy becomes more than a personal attribute. The phenomenon of "collective efficacy" often emerges. This capacity is more than the sum of the perceived self-efficacy of individuals. It is, in addition, the belief in the group's capability to face any threat that arises with a sense of confidence that the group will prevail. In Grundy's previous schools, her faculty and she had a deeply held belief in their ability to accomplish common goals by working effectively together. She built a faculty team of professionals who believed in her and in their joint work. She also hired a core team around her—an assistant principal, school psychologist, and teacher leaders—on whom she could rely. Because of her self-knowledge and confidence, she was able to deliberately hire people who had personality and work styles different from her own but who had strengths in areas where she perceived herself as having weakness. For example, Grundy describes herself as a "big picture" person, so she hired an assistant who is a "detail" person. Building an administrative team with a balance of strengths increased her personal efficacy and resilience capacity and enabled her to weather successfully the myriad of storms, both large and small, that she faced. Berscheid (2003, p. 55) confirms the importance and value of the kind of self-efficacy and social intelligence that Grundy exhibited in enlisting others in her work projects and in developing a work environment with others whose talents complement her own.

Stay Connected to Mentors

Mentors can perform a number of roles. They can provide career advice and even career opportunities. They can offer emotional support as confidantes or practical support as problem solvers. By both how they act and how they think and talk about their actions, mentors also teach you skills and influence your efficacy beliefs.

Modeling the behavior of mentors is an important source of information about your efficacy. Unlike hitters in baseball, for example, who can judge their adequacy from their batting averages, in most school activities, measures of adequacy are less clear. You often can evaluate your proficiency only by comparing yourself to others and convincing yourself that if they can do it, you can, too (Bandura, 1995, p. 86).

Actively seek models who have the competencies to which you aspire and who are similar enough to you that you think modeling is possible (Bandura, 1995, p. 88). Even when your models fail in an activity, if you perceive better alternatives that your model and now you could take, your sense of efficacy may be enhanced.

Just being exposed to effective mentors is not enough to strengthen efficacy, however. Research has identified four cognitive functions that enable modeling to lead to greater efficacy: (1) attending closely not only to what the mentor says and does but also to how your mentor thinks about issues, (2) remembering the complexities of what you want to model, (3) translating these learnings into appropriate actions, and (4) putting them into practice (Bandura, 1995, p. 90).

A high-quality mentoring relationship that enhances the mentee's efficacy and effectiveness, then, is a complex phenomenon that takes time to develop. The level of quality of the relationship strongly correlates with the degree of psychological growth that the mentee experiences (Dutton & Heaphy, 2003, p. 273). This was certainly the case for Betsy Grundy. As a new principal in her previous school, she was assigned a mentor with whom she developed a trusting relationship over a period of years and from whom she learned. The friendship and trust that developed between them enabled Grundy to attend closely to her mentor. As Grundy confronts current problems, even though her mentor has retired and moved away, she often considers how her mentor would think about and solve a problem. She has retained or internalized many of her mentor's perspectives—the "lens" through which her mentor viewed the world. For example, she embraces her mentor's perspectives about student placement. Each parent's job is to get the best possible teacher for his or her child. But the school's job is to create the best possible learning situation for every child. In her professional practice, Grundy has translated this learning from her mentor into a strategy for organizing the annual process for student placement—providing opportunities for parent input but reserving the final decisions for the professionals. Despite the fact that Grundy is now an experienced, midcareer principal, reconnecting with her mentor or finding herself a new one as she encounters new challenges in her new school would be an important step in trying to recover her personal efficacy.

Experienced school leaders whom we interviewed confirmed that mentoring is valuable for mid- or late-career professionals as well as for the new and inexperienced. As he reflected on his career as a superintendent, Canada talked of the value of continued mentoring to sustain and enhance self-efficacy.

"Early on in my professional career," Canada told us, "I listened more to mentors, and I was successful because of that. I now realize that I should have kept the percentage of times I referred to a mentor, to seek advice, more about a 50-50 than I did at the end, when it was probably 70-30. . . . I think that's a mistake on the part of a lot of administrators. As you grow, you tend to believe 'I don't need to seek help.' And [people] are going to say, 'Can't you make a decision?' But as you grow and you take on greater responsibility, you need to have someone whom you interact with outside the system who . . . can honestly tell you what they think is right and wrong. I think there's a great value in that, and I would encourage leaders, administrators, and public educators in particular to maintain that relationship more on a balance."

Canada is describing here a competency trap. That is, as you perceive yourself as more capable, and as your self-confidence strengthens, you may cut yourself off from sources of efficacy-enhancing information. You may perceive the opportunity to learn from mentors and models as a sign of weakness, of low efficacy, rather than as an indicator of strength—that you are self-confident enough to continue to be open to new learning.

School reform experts also recognize the complexity of cognitive functioning involved if mentoring is to affect efficacy when they talk about the importance of long-term mentoring relationships. Dennis

Sparks, for example, told us, "I am a real believer in one-to-one assistance that goes by various names, such as executive coaching, life coaching, where you have regular phone conversations or face-to-face meetings [with someone] who helps you get clear and figure out what you might be able to do to allow you to achieve what is important."

Michael Fullan, too, talked of the importance of mentors in a supportive organizational culture over time: "If you are looking at a given 100 new leaders, you might find 20 percent who couldn't become resilient. They aren't cut out for the complexity. Then you find another chunk at the other end who could take it and run with it, then you have about 60 percent who could get a lot better with messiness if they had the right kind of development . . . So they are going to have a reflecting mentoring relationship with someone in a system who is trying to be culturally more sensitive to complexity and swampiness. If they are in a system that is trying to do that, and if they have the individual qualities and are reflective, and the system is reinforcing it, then things could come together. As I think of time lines, it would take about 10 years to produce a leader who would be good at this."

Among the school leaders whom we interviewed for this volume, some extolled the value of a mentor in the role of model and in other roles as well. Thomas, for example, as a young teacher, had the opportunity to mentor with her district superintendent. "I had a very lucky thing happen to me," she said. "I got a job called administrative assistant to the superintendent, which at that point was a teacher out of the classroom, and you got this year or two years with the superintendent in a learning position. You worked with the board in a gofer kind of capacity, but you went everywhere the superintendent went, including his evaluation. . . . And, as fate would have it, two weeks after I got the job, the superintendent's wife had a heart attack, and I ended up sitting with him at the hospital. I'd bring his mail, stuff to sign, and he and I became very close. After she recovered, the two of them treated me really like their daughter. That ended up being the most wonderful mentoring relationship of all."

Several other interviewees were lucky enough to have bosses who mentored them by helping them to think differently about issues. Maria Goodloe, superintendent of schools in Charleston, South Carolina, talked about her mentoring relationship with her superintendent when she was a high school principal: "He was outspoken, he was a visionary, he was smart, and he was a thinker. . . . Some high school baseball kids did a horrible thing—beating up on kids with baseball bats is something that made me so angry. I was determined they weren't going to walk in graduation. He was so good, he said, 'Now, Maria, I'm not telling you what to do, but I want you to think about this. They've gone through 12 years of school, and this is one incident.' . . . Well, he finally got me to work through it, and he never told me what to do. But I worked through it, and he was right. There was a consequence for their behavior. But it wasn't not allowing them to walk at graduation because to me it fit the crime but it really didn't. It was an overreaction, because it was an emotional incident."

Most of our interviewees talked clearly and consistently of mentors as providing emotional support as well as career opportunities and advice. When Vince Ferrandino, for example, was commissioner of education in Connecticut, the person who hired him and to whom he reported was the then governor, Lowell Weicker. Ferrandino and Weicker collaborated on a plan to equalize and desegregate Connecticut public schools. During the process, Ferrandino, the point man for the plan, ran into stiff opposition that included death threats to himself and his family. Throughout, Ferrandino felt the governor's personal as well as professional support. He describes the governor as much as a counselor and colleague who helped him through this tough time as a political leader to whom he reported: "My basic support was the governor. He was very much aligned with this, supportive, and he would call me on a regular basis to be sure I was OK."

Maintain Strong Workplace Relationships

Your resilient personal efficacy in the face of a life storm generally does not occur in isolation. Translating your efficacy into resilient behavior most frequently occurs in a social context, within a web of your relationships with others. As important as it is to understand the internal strengths and resources that you bring to moments of adversity, it is equally important to understand how the characteristics of relationships affect resilient personal efficacy. What qualities in relationships enable you to persevere in attaining goals in spite of daily challenges, distractions, and setbacks? What qualities in relationships enable you to bounce back from adversity?

Psychologists have only begun to investigate systematically the specific "causal pathways" between strong relationships and psychological strengths like self-efficacy. But they do know that human strengths "reside partly in the interpersonal nets that nurture them" (Caprara & Cervone, 2003, p. 61). Embedded as these strengths are in your social networks, you may possess capacities or potential that only can become realized within particular social situations (p. 65). As Caprara and Cervone state, "A great many of the capacities that you call human strengths derive from the strengths of the communities in which people live" (p. 68).

According to Bandura (1997, p. 101), the primary way that you gain self-efficacy is through "persuasive experiences"—that is, when others who have faith in you persuade you of your capabilities. When others convince you that you can do it, you are likely to try harder, persevere longer, and perform better.

Relationships not only build personal efficacy in this way but also enable quicker and better recovery from setbacks. Reivich and Shatte (2002, p. 24) state that people who are most resilient in bouncing back from trauma exhibit three characteristics: a task-oriented coping style, a confidence that they can control the outcomes of their lives, and an ability to use relationships to cope. These researchers note that resilient people have "strong connections to others" (p. 33). "A lack of connection to others hinders recovery; resilience keeps you connected, and connection helps you heal" (p. 25). A reason, then, that our principal, Betsy Grundy, may have felt more resilient self-efficacy in her first school than she currently feels was that she could turn to trusted colleagues for support in dealing with the storms she faced.

In her previous school, Grundy also learned from and with her faculty. She fondly remembers brainstorming sessions with individuals and groups of teachers in which honest give-and-take occurred. These discussions generated ideas that people fully explored. She and her staff could disagree amicably about them. These sessions resulted in solutions to problems that she would never have discovered by herself. Dutton and Heaphy (2003, p. 266) found that three strengths characterize "high-quality connections" like those between Grundy and her former faculty:

• *Degree of connectivity*—their generativity and openness to new ideas and influences;

- *Higher emotional carrying capacity*—the ability to say anything and get anger and frustration out yet retain trust; and
- *Tensility*—the ability of the relationship to withstand strain, bend with conflict, but not break.

Dutton and Heaphy (p. 267) also found three subjective experiences in high-quality relationships that are consistent with what Grundy felt about her former faculty relationships: feelings of vitality and aliveness, a sense of positive regard, and a felt mutuality.

School reform experts confirm the value and importance of reaching out, developing, and maintaining trusting workplace relationships for enhancing personal efficacy and effectiveness. In our interview, Fullan espoused the kind of caring community that Grundy had established in her previous school. "A culture of care is very important to help a leader move ahead during tough times," he said. "It applies both to the system and to the individual. It is related to moral purpose."

Larry Lezotte suggested that if leaders are to be risk takers, they may need to bring trusted allies with them when they change jobs. "People are less willing to take risks alone than they are together. . . . I think so much of resilience is about relationships. Most people need to have colleagues also share in the struggle. If they don't, then it is very hard. That's why some people as superintendents find it necessary to take someone with them, because they need to have a touchstone in their new place." Grundy's superintendent did not offer the opportunity to bring members of her core administrative team with her to her new school. Perhaps if he had, her efficacy and effectiveness in her new school might be more positive.

Finally, Sparks talked about how to build trusting relationships at work: "Being a committed listener, being one of these people whom others feel they can speak candidly to without punishment and who will really hear them. . . . People say things in public meetings that demand the very best of you to hear the anger and not respond in kind or internalize the anger and have it to destroy your body or your relationships."

In their practice, effective school leaders have learned to be "committed listeners" and to develop and maintain strong, trusting relationships on which they can rely, especially during times of crisis. Thomas described such a moment early in her elementary principalship in the

North East School District in San Antonio. At a meeting that she did not attend, a number of faculty expressed concern over the vision and direction of the school, she told us. "But I had a teacher—we'd known each other a long time. She came back after school, after all the meetings and everybody was gone, and came into my office and said, 'I need to tell you something.' And she told me. I've learned that principals aren't going to know a lot. There are a lot of things you won't know simply because you sit in that chair. And you depend on people you trust to tell you the truth. And you'd better be ready to listen." Because Thomas had this trusting relationship and was "a committed listener," she received essential, though painful, feedback. With her efficacy beliefs intact, Thomas was then able to plan and facilitate a constructive, safe faculty discussion where people could speak candidly without fear of retribution. The meeting became the first step in an ongoing process that strengthened collective efficacy and changed her school.

In talking of the power of relationships, the superintendents whom we interviewed often focused on the importance of a supportive board of education. In describing the breadth of change in Beaufort, South Carolina, during his superintendency, including opening 10 new schools in response to growing enrollment, Herman Gaither discussed how he and the district have coped successfully: "The board's been very supportive in helping us meet the needs of all of our communities. It will be doubly difficult if you have to spend as much energy trying to keep your board in line as you do in trying to solve your problems. It is much more beneficial to everyone when the board and the administration have the same goals and the same direction."

When board members become members of the caring community, superintendents thrive. Carol Choye said of her board in Scotch Plains, New Jersey, "They go out of their way to be kind and supportive. Now this may sound crazy, but they even give me birthday presents! I mean, they are so kind and so thoughtful."

Effective school leaders strengthen the support they receive from workplace relationships by changing "I" experiences into "we" experiences. Overcoming feelings of isolation and loneliness can be enormously efficacy enhancing. Canada talked about his efforts to reach out from the organizational isolation of his office as superintendent.

"To deal with the loneliness and the stress of being in this high-demand, low-support arena," he said, "one of the things that I would do was, once a month I'd hand-sign birthday cards to everybody in the district. And the cards were created from student artwork we had selected and printed up that month, and I used it. It was just a small token on my part to personally say, 'I've taken the time to say I know this is your birthday, and here's a card from me to say happy birthday to you.' It made me feel good; it also helped the other people feel good. . . . By the same token, I shook the hand of every graduate. Ten high schools, and I did that for every district I was in for every graduation, including alternative schools. A lot of handshakes!" In a "high-demand, low-support" job, these strategies helped Canada feel connected to others and more efficacious.

Maintain Strong Personal Relationships

Relationships with people outside the workplace are also vital to maintaining and strengthening personal efficacy. In their book *The Power of Full Engagement,* Loehr and Schwartz (2003) describe how. "The pulse of strong relationships"—involving giving and taking, valuing and feeling valued—nourishes and renews. These relationships create a "reservoir of positive emotional energy" on which a person can then draw at work (pp. 81, 82). From this perspective, we can be realistically optimistic about Principal Grundy's chances of regaining her effectiveness and emerging with even stronger resilient self-efficacy. She has a long-term, supportive life partner. And she has close friends outside school in whom she can also confide.

Among the accomplished professionals we interviewed, several described how personal relationships sustained their personal efficacy during times of crisis. Roland Barth talked of his battle with prostate cancer: "I knew three or four friends who had prostate cancer and had been receiving treatment. I got on the e-mail and asked them questions about procedures. All of a sudden I went from 'I' to a 'we.' And in schools, if you can get a 'we,' there is something much more comprehensible about the condition. These guys were really role models for me. I have subsequently become the support system for two or three other friends who were diagnosed after me, just having the 'we' and sharing the same maladies." Changing the "I" to "we" is efficacy enhancing in personal as well as professional life.

When Bandura (1997, p. 106) talks about "persuasive experiences" that shape your self-efficacy, he is not describing "pep talks" that you may have received along the way in life. Instead, he means early influences, such as parents, who verbally instill in children self-belief in their own potential and power. He argues that these individuals can have a lasting effect on personal efficacy beliefs. School leaders to whom we talked had rich stories about powerful parental influence on their self-confidence. Maria Goodloe recalled, for example, "When I was little . . . I was quiet and shy. . . . But there was a distinctive experience I remember. We went to get ice cream. . . . My mother wasn't with me—she waited in the car. . . . And people went in and came out, went in and came out. What was happening was, adults were doing 'adultism,' and they weren't allowing me to get in line to make my order. I just took it; I just stood there. And so finally she came in and said, 'What are you doing? Six people have come in after you and left.' . . . So she taught me from that day on: 'You need to speak up. You don't have to be rude, but you don't let people do that to you. Say, *Excuse me, but I was next.* And say it loud enough to get people's attention, but you don't have to be rude.' " Goodloe's ice cream store experience with "adultism" was obviously a "persuasive experience" that has had a lasting impact on her personal efficacy beliefs.

Other school leaders also talked about parents and grandparents who shaped their self-efficacy and other human strengths. Paul Houston, in discussing his research about spirituality in leadership, for example, describes the source of optimism: "Where does optimism come from? What we concluded was that you had to have at least one parent who loved you unconditionally." Alicia Thomas reflected on adaptability by remembering her grandmother: "I think back on the things she had to deal with in her life," she said, "and she just adjusted to the situation and to the people she was with. . . . This [was] one of the secrets of her life."

Intimate partners and family clearly help sustain the human strengths, including personal efficacy, of school leaders in demanding jobs. Several interviewees commented on the importance to their psychological health of maintaining a balance between work and family commitments. As we described in Chapter 4, Gene Carter told us about his family council in which each person, even his children, had a vote about whether he should make a career move.

Some school leaders remember people outside their families who believed in them. Carter, again, recalled the owner of a clothing store where he worked as a teenager who encouraged him to go to college at a time when it was not "routine . . . for kids in that community to go on to college." They developed a relationship that helped sustain Carter over several years. Several other school leaders recalled teachers and members of the clergy who had a formative influence on their self-efficacy beliefs. Goodloe recognized that organizational responsibilities can sometimes burden a personal relationship and jeopardize confidentiality. She, and others, advocate outside friendships. "I had great friends in Corpus Christi that I met and just clicked, and they've always supported me," she said. "So I could always go and talk to them and cry and be mad and be angry and say certain things that you can't say at work or to people because you know it's inappropriate. And I always got through it."

Summary: Nine Strategies to Translate Efficacy Beliefs into Action

Our research has identified two key building blocks of efficacy that can help you strengthen your beliefs about your capability to survive, thrive, and be resilient in the face of storms. We have also described nine strategies to translate your personal efficacy into effective action. We close this chapter by summarizing them.

Strengthen Competence and Confidence

- *Build your sense of mastery,* as Linda Hanson has done, to appraise your experience and to learn from it, to become more "grounded" in what is important, and to become more self-reflective.
- *Set short-term goals and benchmarks of progress,* following the example of Carol Choye, to chunk out long-term, complex plans into manageable increments that will help you sustain motivation, avoid distractions, and recognize success.
- *Claim small wins,* as did our principal, Betsy Grundy, to sustain efficacy over time.
- *Recover quickly from setbacks,* as Ben Canada and Alicia Thomas have, to keep a bump in the road from becoming a major pothole.
- *Manage yourself,* especially your emotional self-control, so that you can maximize the benefits of positive emotions and lessen the costs of negative feelings.

Maintain and Increase Strong Connections to Others

• *Believe in the power of team,* as Grundy did in her previous school, and let faith in the capability of your colleagues sustain you in moments of personal doubt and uncertainty.

• *Stay connected to mentors,* as so many of our interviewees have done. Avoid the "competency trap" that assumes that seeking advice and help is a sign of weakness.

• *Maintain strong workplace relationships,* again as many of our interviewees have done, turning to trusted friends and confidantes at work for counsel and support during storms.

• *Maintain strong personal relationships* to sustain personal efficacy over time.

8

THE MEANING AND IMPORTANCE OF PERSONAL ENERGY

Energy is your capacity to do work. It provides the fuel that enables you to weather the storm effectively and to bounce back resiliently. You may have strong and clear core values, and you may have an equally strong sense of efficacy. But, if you cannot translate those attributes into action, then they come to naught. Transforming your values and beliefs into resilient behavior depends on your energy capacity and your energy expenditure and recovery patterns.

Energy is essential to effective leadership. In your role, you not only need to stay personally energized but also must energize others. Your colleagues must feel committed to the vision for the future that you and they have collaboratively pictured, and they must feel motivated to work to make that vision a reality.

In this chapter, we will discuss the importance of energy to you personally and to you as a leader. We will explain sources of both personal and organizational energy; discuss ways that you can expand your energy; and present strategies for effective energy management, recovery, and leadership.

The Importance of Energy

You may think that, besides money, your most significant personal resource in your professional and personal life is time. "I have too much to do and not enough time to do it" is a familiar complaint that we frequently express in moments of frustration. As organized as you may be, if you are like most highly motivated, competent professionals, you probably sit with a "to do" list of tasks awaiting completion as a burden of varying weight on your shoulders. You may have learned to take pride in "multi-tasking" as you juggle the items on your list. And you may accept that your job is "24/7," even though that description implies that your work never ends and that you do not have a time to recover from the demands of work or to have a personal life. The irony is that the most capable people are the most apt to feel this frustration. Because you are good at what you do, you generate more work, either through your own initiative or that of others who recognize your value. Barry Jentz, author and management consultant, describes this work-world phenomenon as "opportunity madness." It describes a condition of vulnerability faced by achievement-oriented, successful people who constantly create or are offered alluring opportunities to get involved in a project, event, or idea that will require more of their time and energy when they are already overextended.

Time is, of course, finite and is often a major resource constraint particularly if you underestimate how much time a new opportunity requires and overcommit yourself by voluntarily adding it to your "to do" list. However, another perspective on the constraints you face on your personal resources is that the most significant problem is not time but energy. In *The Power of Full Engagement,* Loehr and Schwartz (2003) argue that managing energy, not time, is the key to high performance and personal renewal. Though time is finite, the quality and quantity of your energy are not. Your energy "tank" can be empty or overflowing depending, at least in part, on your ability to manage your energy expenditure and recovery effectively. When your energy is depleted or when you are distracted and unable to focus your energy on the task at hand, you do not perform at your best. Conversely, the more you are able to enhance the quality and quantity of your energy, the more productive, healthier, and happier you will be.

Sources of Energy

To be fully engaged, you must effectively maximize four key types of energy: physical, emotional, mental, and spiritual (Loehr & Schwartz, 2003, p. 9). Tapping your reserves of all four types of energy and increasing available energy of each type are critical to your happiness and success. You need energy of all four types because as a human being, you are a complex energy system in which the "mind and body are one" (p. 11). Moreover, each energy type influences the other. When you have all four working for you positively and actively, you can achieve a state of "full engagement" and perform at your peak (p. 9).

Full engagement is like the state of consciousness that athletes call "the zone," in which you can focus all your attention and concentration on the challenge at hand, your emotions are positive and aligned with your work, and you feel relaxed and intent but not anxious. Time slows down in the zone, or you lose track of it altogether. Mihaly Csikszentmihalyi, a psychologist who has studied peak performance for more than two decades, calls this state "flow" (as cited in Goleman, 1995). Daniel Goleman, author of *Emotional Intelligence,* describes it as a "master aptitude" (p. 95) of effective people.

When you are not fully engaged, conversely, you may feel "split." You may not be fully present in the moment. You may feel emotions triggered by a memory or a prior experience. You may also feel distracted and listless, unable to concentrate fully on the people or problem at hand. When you feel split, your performance cannot be your best. Going into a meeting while you are still churning emotionally or mentally about unresolved issues in a previous meeting is a good example of being split. Your emotions may not be aligned with your experiences in the second meeting. If your emotional affect is obviously not in alignment, people may even ask you what is wrong.

Increasing all four types of energy capacity occurs when you push beyond your energy expenditure limits and then cycle through a period of recovery. Just as world-class athletes stretch their strength, speed, or endurance by pushing beyond physical limits into pain and discomfort, and then by providing themselves the nurturance and rest necessary for recovery, you should stretch your energy limits to increase capacity (Loehr & Schwartz, 2003, p. 9). Rather than seeing stress as a discomfort and to be avoided at all costs or as a ceaseless, negative by-product of challenging work to be suffered interminably, you can turn stress to your advantage. "We grow at all levels by expending energy beyond our ordinary limits and then recovering" (p. 13). Though stress causes discomfort and pain, it also enables you to expand your physical, emotional, mental, and spiritual energy capacity. The key, again, to stress having a healthy outcome is that it should be followed by adequate rest and recovery. For example, a late board meeting might warrant a late start to the next day's schedule or a hectic workweek with several late nights could be followed by a "down" weekend.

Physical Fuel

Physical energy is the underlying source of fuel for all dimensions of your performance. It affects your feelings of vitality and alertness, your ability to manage your emotions, and your mental sharpness, creativity, motivation, and commitment. The size of your energy reserves depends on what and how you eat, the amount you sleep, and your level of fitness. Research suggests that certain rituals produce the largest energy resources: eating five to six low-calorie and high-nutrition meals each day, drinking 64 ounces of water, sleeping seven to eight hours, and engaging in interval training as a regular form of physical exercise (Loehr & Schwartz, 2003). Demanding work schedules on top of family or other personal commitments can easily lead to neglect of these healthy rituals. You may try to get by with less sleep, without exercise, or without taking the time to eat a healthy meal. Remember that your health, vitality, and energy are your own most precious resources and among your organization's most precious resources.

Emotional Mastery

Positive emotions increase energy and your ability to manage all your feelings, including the negative ones. Joy, enthusiasm, and happiness release energy that is essential to peak performance. According to Goleman (1995, p. 7), happiness stimulates activity in the brain center that inhibits negative emotion and increases energy and enthusiasm for new tasks and ambitious goals. In contrast, sadness reduces energy and enthusiasm. When it reaches depression, it actually slows the body's metabolism.

Quinn and Dutton define energy as a positive emotion. They say it is "a type of positive affective arousal, which people experience as emotion—short responses to specific events—or mood—longer lasting affective states that need not be a response to a specific event" (cited in Baker, Cross, & Wooten, 2003, p. 331).

Loehr and Schwartz (2003) also describe this link between energy and emotion. Whereas positive emotions fuel energy, when negative emotions such as anger, defensiveness, and depression overwhelm you, they deplete energy stores rapidly and undermine your ability to perform at your best. Loehr and Schwartz cite as an example John McEnroe's explanation of his loss to Ivan Lendl in the1984 French Open in which he said that he "wasted too much energy being angry" (p. 75). If experienced chronically, negative emotions may not only slow the body's responses but be physically debilitating. Research has consistently found, for example, that chronic depression doubles the likelihood of Alzheimer's disease.

Emotional intelligence provides "the capacity to manage emotions skillfully in the service of high positive energy and full engagement" (Loehr & Schwartz, 2003, p. 72). In contrast, when emotional intelligence is lower, you are less aware of your emotional responses, less able to manage negative impulses and emotions, and less empathetic to others.

Goleman (1995) tells us "all emotions are, in essence, impulses to act, the instant plans for handling life that evolution instilled in us" (p. 6). As products of the limbic system, which is the nonverbal part of the brain, they bypass the rational brain. Researchers have documented how emotions immediately produce physiological responses that prepare us to act. Anger, for example, increases blood flow and heart rate, triggers hormones like adrenaline, and "generates a pulse of energy strong enough for vigorous action" (p. 6). In an instant, these impulses can overwhelm rational thought processes and judgment.

As this anger example suggests, some people are, at least sometimes, overcome by their emotions. Managing these impulses, then, is a key element of emotional intelligence and emotional mastery. Goleman (1995, p. 47) states that emotional self-awareness is the foundation stone of emotional competence, including impulse control. Because emotions arise from the limbus, conscious awareness of your emotions is not a given. Some of us are "passion's slaves" (p. 56), acting on emotions without thought or judgment. Others of us seem hardly aware that our emotions exist and have a "flat" affect. In this category, Loehr and Schwartz cite clients who experience a lack of depth in their emotional relationships in the workplace and at home. Understanding that you feel and clarity about what you feel are critical to being able to manage your emotions constructively. "An inability to notice our true feelings leaves us at their mercy" (Goleman, 1995, p. 43).

Empathy and other social skills that build on self-awareness as well as inner-directed abilities and attitudes like self-awareness, self-efficacy, and self-control define your emotional intelligence and fuel positive emotions and energy. The more attuned you are to your own feelings, the more sensitive you will be to the feelings of others (Goleman, 1995, p. 96).

According to Goleman, another key element of emotional intelligence is managing mood—especially gloominess, irritability, and melancholy. You cannot necessarily control what negative feelings come over you or when you feel them, but you can influence how long you feel bad (p. 57). One strategy for managing negative feelings is, first, to recognize and acknowledge explicitly to yourself that you are feeling bad. Then, consciously try to replace the negative thoughts that accompany the negative feelings with positive thoughts—perhaps remembering a past success and the strengths that it confirmed. The ability to shake off negative emotions quickly enables you to feel more energetic and resilient. You bounce back sooner from the effects of life's storms. In contrast, those who constantly struggle with the negative often feel split in focus and depleted of energy.

Your response to the trauma and pain of life's storms can also expand your emotional energy. You can heal in the broken places and actually be stronger. From their work, Loehr and Schwartz cite the example of a client who worked near the World Trade Center and lost many friends in the 9/11 disaster. Afterward, he felt traumatized and unable to resume his normal life. But rituals—daily physical workouts and playtimes with his daughter—provided a source of emotional recovery, as did dozens of memorial services for lost friends. Though sad and difficult, these services became celebrations of life that enabled him to heal and recover.

Mental Focus

You need mental energy to focus and to concentrate. It is essential to full engagement and high performance. The most valuable mental energy is realistic optimism—perceiving reality accurately but at the same time focusing clearly and steadfastly on goals that make it better (see Chapters 2 and 3).

As with other forms of energy, you can develop your mental energy capacity by balancing energy expenditure with energy recovery (Loehr & Schwartz, 2003, p. 109). Increasing evidence indicates that the brain operates like a muscle, developing its powers in the face of new challenges and atrophying with lack of use throughout life. "The brain gets sharper the more it's used" (p. 101). This phenomenon is especially important as you age. Stretching your mental capacity can offset age-related mental decline.

As with emotional energy, physical energy fuels mental energy. The problem is that thinking or rational analysis requires a great deal of mental energy. Though the brain is only 2 percent of your body weight, it uses 25 percent of your oxygen supply. Energy recovery, then, is critical. Loehr and Schwartz argue that regular workplace breaks are necessary to maintain full engagement and high performance. Citing Michael Gelb's *How to Think Like Leonardo da Vinci,* they point out that you probably get your best ideas someplace other than at your desk working. They come to you in the shower or in bed or while you are working out (p. 96). These recovery activities clearly generate renewed mental energy.

Loehr and Schwartz also suggest that mental energy recovery depends on alternating "mental channels" (p. 94). Specifically, they cite research showing that use of the right hemisphere of the brain in creative activities provides time for recovery for the left hemisphere, which we need for the rational, analytic activity that predominates in the workplace.

The Spiritual Wellspring

Goleman (1995) as well as Loehr and Schwartz (2003) describe motivation as a key to positive energy, resilience, and effectiveness. It enables you to marshal emotion toward a goal and strengthens perseverance and persistence in the face of adversity. Motivation arises from your commitment to your deepest values. These values, then, are a wellspring of spiritual energy.

We use the term *wellspring* to describe the source of spiritual energy because most educators have a deep energy reserve in the values that drive their work and their reasons for choosing to be educators. Robert N. Bellah has suggested three orientations to work. For many people, work is merely a job, a way to make a living. For many others, work is a career, an opportunity for advancement and reward. Finally, for some, work is a calling, an opportunity for fulfillment of values (cited in Wrzesniewski, 2003, p. 301). From our experience and our research, we think most educators fall into this third category. Your sense of mission is a strong and deep spiritual energy reserve.

Reconnecting with your values at critical moments can expand energy capacity. Thompson (2004) talks of the importance of a leader finding or creating the "eye of the storm," a retreat in the midst of the tumult where you can renew your spiritual energy. Thompson gives examples of school leaders who, while besieged by other people's anger and frustration, stepped back and reconnected with their deeper selves— their personal sense of mission or their core values. For the leaders whom Thompson cites, these eye-of-the-storm moments brought peace, clarified events, altered their perspectives, and renewed their motivation and conviction.

If you have an underdeveloped spiritual capacity, you may have lost your sense of purpose or the passion you once felt for your work. To renew your spirit, and to strengthen your motivation and commitment to purpose, you need to remind yourself regularly of the values that are the most meaningful to you, those that reflect purposes beyond your own self-interest (see Chapters 4 and 5 for more on core values).

Energy Management

Managing your personal energy and holding yourself responsible for how you manage it are just as important as holding yourself responsible for managing other precious personal and organizational resources, such as money and time.

Responsible energy management means expanding your sources of energy, as previously discussed. It also means providing yourself with sufficient energy recovery after an interval of energy expenditure, as we will discuss in the next section. In addition to these activities, if you are an effective energy manager, you have several other characteristic strategies. First, you are adept at transforming negative energy into positive energy. Without being labeled a Pollyanna, you can find the silver lining in any cloud. Second, you make wise decisions about where and how you choose to invest energy, avoiding wasting energy on less important, peripheral issues. Third, your hope, conviction, and motivation are sufficiently strong that you persist in expending energy through the storm in order to reach the sunlight on the other side. In other words, you do not give up prematurely. As we have said earlier, resilience can mean giving up an unsuccessful strategy without giving up its goal and then developing a new strategy. Poor energy managers, however, waste energy by investing it and then giving up before it has a chance to yield an outcome. We give examples of these energy management characteristics in the next chapter when we discuss how school leaders sustain and increase energy.

Energy management, finally, means that you can find the eye-of-the-storm moments that Thompson describes. This kind of adaptive distancing enables you to keep a sense of self as an autonomous being amid the chaos. Otherwise, the storm can be overwhelming—with the events themselves and the cacophony of opinions of others about the events defining what a leader says, does, and even thinks.

Energy Recovery

To manage energy effectively and to be fully engaged, you must, first, allow time for energy recovery after you have expended bursts of energy. You may assume that your energy stores are limitless and push yourself well beyond the point where you can perform at your peak. This approach to unending energy expenditure robs you of the resources you need for effective performance. Workaholics who end up feeling burned out, depressed, and disengaged from their work personify the dangers of this linear approach. It is not the intensity of their work that produces burnout but the "duration of expenditure without recovery" (Loehr & Schwartz, 2003, p. 41).

To avoid burnout, you must adopt a cyclical, dynamic approach to energy expenditure and recovery. Loehr and Schwartz suggest that you live your life not as marathoners do. Marathoners' faces and bodies look pained, gaunt, and drained of energy as they run on and on, perhaps to the point of collapse. Instead, you should live your life as sprinters do. They look powerful, robust, and "eager to push themselves to their limits" as they look forward to the next short but intense burst of energy (p. 12). To live like a sprinter, you need to break the tasks of life down into manageable increments that meet your needs to alternate energy expenditure and recovery.

The work–rest cycle is perhaps most obvious in the physical domain, but it is essential for "full engagement" in other dimensions as well. Emotional mastery depends on developing your capacity for active engagement with others and contemplative reflection with your own feelings. Mental sharpness depends on finding new intellectual challenges and making the time for "no-brainer" kinds of activities such as watching television, listening to music, and exercising. Spiritual energy depends on regular reconnections with your core values. Each type of energy requires a "dynamic balance between the expenditure of energy (stress) and the renewal of energy (recovery) in all dimensions" (p. 29).

How do you change your behavior to incorporate more energy recovery? Changing behavior is incredibly difficult. We are all creatures of habit. "What we did yesterday is what we are likely to do today" (p. 14). What's more, the will and discipline necessary to break habits and make changes in how you behave are themselves limited resources. You cannot depend on them to sustain over time what you resolve to do differently.

Loehr and Schwartz argue that, instead, you must create "positive rituals," which they define as specific behaviors that you perform at specific times. In other words, if you are to manage your energy more effectively toward the goal of better performance, then you must create new habits. If energy recovery for you means some time alone in the middle of every day to recharge your batteries, then you need to schedule a specific activity at a specific time for it to occur—for example, a walk at lunch or a midafternoon meditation break in your office with the lights off and door closed.

Technological advances such as fax machines and e-mail have both quickened the pace of work and made its reach more pervasive in our lives. In this new work environment, it is even more critical that we find ways to disengage from the 24/7 pace. As Loehr and Schwartz argue, "we must learn to establish stopping points in our days, inviolable times when we step off the track, cease processing information, and shift our attention from achievement to restoration" (p. 39).

The alternating cycle of work and recovery does not have to span hours or days. In his research, Jim Loehr found that world-class tennis players have a remarkable capacity to renew energy in the time between points in a match. They tend to follow exactly the same rituals between points (e.g., staring at the strings on their rackets). In some cases, during these between-point rituals, their heartbeats drop by as many as 20 beats per minute (p. 32). Effective "corporate athletes," in Loehr and Schwartz's research, also have developed rituals at work for quick recovery, such as walking through their office and talking with people, or simply drinking a bottle of water. Merely changing the pattern of your breathing by extending exhalation can produce "a powerful wave of recovery" (p. 49).

As these examples suggest, you can engage in "intermittent recovery" during the workday. Research has shown that your physical energy ebbs and flows in cycles of 90 to 120 minutes throughout your waking day. Sometime toward the end of a cycle in which you have been focused on a task, your body begins to look for a period of rest and recovery. You feel restless; you stretch; you yawn; you start to feel hungry; you have more difficulty concentrating; you are more prone to mistakes. You can override these signals and keep working, but at a cost. You have to call on stress hormones to energize yourself in the short term. As we said in the previous chapter, evidence indicates that these hormones may actually be physically addictive. And they also produce other, negative long-term consequences, including both negative emotions and physical maladies (Loehr & Schwartz, 2003, p. 31).

In considering rituals to help build emotional capacity and enhance emotional recovery so that you become more resilient, Loehr and Schwartz (p. 79) advise that you explore activities that at some point in your life have given you deep pleasure and satisfaction. These experiences tend to create positive emotions. If you can build them into daily or at least regular rituals, you build emotional reserves that can increase your effectiveness. If earlier in life, for example, you enjoyed reading novels for pleasure but rarely have the time now, you might consider a daily ritual where you leave your office and sit somewhere pleasant and read for 45 minutes. The consequence may be that you are more able to support and help those with whom you work or live.

Perhaps a more substantive example of rituals to increase emotional capacity involves forming workplace friendships. Research has shown that high-quality workplace relationships can be energizing both physically and psychologically. Energizing relationships lead people to feel more physically aware, intent, and attuned to their surroundings. They also lead to more cognitive engagement and the ability to think better and faster. Finally, people report that energizing relationships are tremendously motivational (Baker, Cross & Wooten, 2003, pp. 332, 333). Loehr and Schwartz (p. 81) cite Gallup's research that found that a key factor in sustained workplace performance was having at least one good friend. Such friendship involves both energy expenditure—giving to, listening to, and valuing the other person—and energy recovery—taking from, being listened to, and being valued in return.

In addition to energizing workplace relationships, personal relationships can also be energizing. Another example of devising rituals to develop more positive energy involves investing more time and energy in key people in your personal life. Rituals such as scheduling a weeknight date with your spouse or weekly time alone with your child can increase positive emotion and workplace energy.

These positive rituals can enable you to transform your core values and your efficacy beliefs into new sources of energy that produce effective action. Loehr and Schwartz suggest that before establishing new routines in your life, you should ask yourself, "How should I spend my energy in a way that is consistent with my deepest values?" The link that we create between values and new rituals "fuels a uniquely high-octane source of energy for change" (p. 16).

Energy Leadership

School leaders are "energy creators" (Fullan, 2001, p. 149). Your effectiveness involves managing not only your own feelings, focus, and attitudes to produce positive energy but also those of others. You must be able "to mobilize and inspire others, . . . to persuade and influence, to put others at their ease" (Goleman, 1995, p. 113). The importance of your energy-creating ability is hard to overstate. Mobilizing energy and inspiring efforts are absolutely critical to the deep changes in school climate and culture that you probably want to make. For example, Loehr and Schwartz (2003) cite research by Gallup that the relationship between an employee and the boss is the best predictor of productivity. If employees feel that the boss cares for them and believes in them, they perform better.

To be an effective leader, you must use positive energy to communicate effectively and empathetically with those you lead, to nurture their self-efficacy, to support their growth and ability to respond to workplace challenges. The need for you to have reserves of positive energy is especially acute during periods of intense stress, when the organization faces the threat of storms. One of your key roles is to enable followers to transform the negative emotional response (e.g., fear that the threat may generate) into the positive emotional responses (e.g., excitement at a new opportunity) that create the full engagement of high performance. As you will see in the next chapter, experienced and effective school leaders demonstrate strategies for enabling this transformation.

9

How Leaders Sustain and Increase Energy

Energy depletion and exhaustion are significant dangers for any school leader. The needs confronting you in schools are compelling, and the demands that you must meet are urgent. By their nature, schools are places for givers. And by your nature, you are a person willing to make extraordinary commitments. During our interviews for this book, we heard many stories of commitment that went far above and beyond what anyone could reasonably expect. For example, Carol Choye was on sick leave, between cancer surgery and radiation, when a female student was assaulted by five boys behind the middle school, a story that hit the *New York Times.* Choye left her sickbed to handle that emergency. In an example mentioned in chapter 5, when a 7th grade girl threatened suicide, Choye chose to drive the girl and her family to a child psychiatric facility because other staff were unavailable and the only other options were to send the family in a taxi or wait until the next day. In our research, stories like these are not unique to Choye, nor are they atypical of school leaders. In fact, they are emblematic. Nearly every one of our interviewees told such stories.

This willingness to give is truly admirable. But it carries with it the danger that continuous energy expenditure leaves school leaders exhausted, depressed, and unable to perform effectively. School administration, as Ben Canada characterized the superintendency, is a "high-demand, low-support arena." Coping with the energy depletion, loneliness, and stress that result from these conditions challenges every administrator's mettle. The purpose of this chapter is to help you rise to the challenge.

Physical Reserves

Harnessing physical energy means ensuring that you have enough of it. As we explained in Chapter 8, physical energy is the underlying fuel for all dimensions of your performance. All our interviewees struggled with the physical strain of a 24/7 job and the ceaseless demands for energy expenditure. Nearly all of them talked about the importance of taking care of themselves physically and replenishing their fuel cells by getting enough rest, eating well, and exercising. We discuss the need for physical recovery strategies, with examples from our research, in the "Energy Recovery" section later.

Emotional Energy

Harnessing emotional energy demands the capacity to manage emotions skillfully in order to maximize positive energy and outcomes. Our interviewees also displayed sophisticated emotional intelligence, the quality that enables you to develop and sustain the positive energy that produces positive emotions. Linda Hanson, for example, demonstrated the self-awareness that is the foundation of emotional intelligence (Goleman, 1995, p. 47). You will recall from chapter 7 that when we asked her about her strengths, she talked of trusting her own instincts, what she had learned about herself from her experience. She was confident enough in her own self-knowledge to use herself "as a laboratory" when evaluating a proposal she was considering.

Ben Canada, too, emphasized the importance of self-awareness. "We first have to not only know who we are but we have to learn what our capacity is, what our capabilities are, 'what can I do, and do I have the time to do it?' so that you don't create unrealistic expectations or make unrealistic promises."

Alicia Thomas told us about developing greater self-awareness in response to adversity. As a young principal, she had a conflict with a teacher that she found upsetting. She turned to books to try "to figure out why I was so upset." Through reading, she came to understand more about herself, especially the reflexive behaviors from childhood that persist in everyone's adulthood and can affect workplace performance.

School leaders sometimes use creative strategies to enhance their emotional intelligence. Hanson described what she did when she realized that she needed better ways to manage her emotions "when I feel I'm being pushed. And I can feel that I'm getting mad and my temper is getting up." She decided to do some action research. She interviewed the 15 people in her district who others said were able to manage anger well, stay positive, and handle conflict. She heard at least 25 strategies. Interestingly, some were things that she had sometimes done but never articulated. Once they were explicit rather than tacit, she was able to use them more readily.

As we would expect from successful school leaders, our interviewees revealed impressive emotional capacity—a broad repertoire of social skills. Among the most valuable is the ability, as Herman Gaither said, "to disarm opponents, not fight with them." Sometimes in schools as in nature, the wisest course is to recognize that the storm just must be weathered. The controversy will swirl and cause temporary disruption, but it will end. Simply riding out the storm will enable the proposed change to occur. Lynne Shain described how just waiting (deferring a decision) can bring this success: During the implementation phase of a new elementary science program, principals complained that teachers were experiencing "meltdown" trying to cope with too many new responsibilities. They urged that the second unit in the project be delayed. Shain had an intuition that impending parent conferences were making teachers "edgy." She said to the principals, "Let's not make a decision today. Let's wait until our next meeting in two weeks." Two weeks later, complaints had subsided, and implementation proceeded on schedule.

Managing communication toward positive ends during emotionally tense interactions is another valuable social skill. Shain mentioned the importance of being able to "think about what you're saying before it comes out of your mouth," as she put it. She described how she "studies" her words and "washes them" to avoid expressing a negative message.

To manage his emotions and maintain his composure in potentially volatile public situations, such as board meetings, Canada "made it a point to look up frequently directly in the eye of the person who was speaking and try to show a face of concern and yet in total control. And I would smile a lot. At the point where the person may have been showing their greatest level of hostility and anger, I may have a small smile on my face and I knew that it was irritating the person, but it was my way of maintaining my composure."

The harsh reality that life springs surprises can test any leader's emotional capacity. In Chapter 3, we described how Hanson tried to embrace surprise and reduce its ability to create fear, anger, and other negative emotions. Indeed, one of her planning strategies was to build the anticipation of surprises into the plan and to counsel her staff to welcome them. According to Hanson, "We will come away a little bit different because of a disruption or a surprise we have to process. So let's just build it in and expect it to happen. And it always does happen. Almost always I think, even though [the unexpected] can be tedious, and it can feel like it's slowing your progress down, it is something good that comes of a disruption or a surprise. . . . If you think of it as just a part of the process and think of it as typical rather than atypical, you probably have a better ability to live with it."

Mental Focus

Harnessing mental energy involves finding and keeping focus. Our research suggests that clarity about values and goals enables concentration and focus while reducing the likelihood of distraction. Exploring ideas can also stimulate and expand your mental energy.

The Role of Clear Goals and Values

You cannot stay mentally focused and directed if you are unclear about where you are going, what the goal is, and why it is important. Similarly, many of our interviewees talked about the importance of discovering what values they hold most dear in order to develop and maintain mental focus. Without this awareness, conflict and controversy can erode self-confidence and produce negative emotions that debilitate energy.

As we mentioned in chapter 4, Hanson had not yet fully determined her educational values early in her career. She felt "not grounded," unsure about the direction that her leadership should provide. She questioned whether what she was doing was best for kids and felt the erosion of positive energy that results from lack of confidence. She described herself then as more event driven than value driven. With experience, she became "grounded," able to base her leadership on an explicit set of beliefs about teaching and learning. She described how through experience she developed an explicit values framework that she shared with her staff and board. This framework provided a "context for conversations" and stimulated the positive energy and confidence that produced good decisions based on those values. "When I talk to other administrators," she commented, "those who are not well grounded in philosophy, who do not know what they believe about teaching and learning and what they believe about kids—I find them having a much more difficult time than people who really know what they believe."

Knowing what you believe also enables you to feel validation and success when you act in accord with values. Those positive feelings stimulate more energy. Chuck Fowler described a time when a controversial open-enrollment plan that he had initiated enabled small groups of students to transfer middle schools each year and make a fresh start. Students benefited without any overcrowding, the risk that others had feared and predicted, occurring. Fowler was able to savor the success of his values-based decision. "You never say anything, but you just have a smile in your heart," he said.

When your values and goals are clear, you can take the long view in the face of a storm. This ability may be the first step toward energy recovery from what might otherwise be a crushing setback. When we interviewed Jo Moffett, superintendent of schools in Greenburgh, New York, she had just suffered a critical defeat of a grade-level realignment proposal. Despite the obvious pain of this setback and the uneasiness of still being immersed in an unsettled controversy, she was able to affirm her long-term success in the district. Whatever the political fallout from this event, she knew that she had made the district "a better place."

This perspective-taking ability enables school leaders to relieve some of the sting of negative media coverage that otherwise can sap personal morale and energy. Moffett was able to say "As horrible as it is . . . it will pass. The newspapers will stop writing about it. It'll stop running on Channel 12."

Hanson has developed a seven-day perspective on newspaper controversies. When she was feeling personally vulnerable and exposed because of a "stupid quote in the newspaper," she would say to herself, "Last time, in seven days it was over. So I'm going to give myself seven days and to the extent possible not dwell on it. Then, I'm going to revisit it and see how I feel." Almost always, by the next week, her perspective was different.

Staying focused on core values also enables school leaders to avoid distracting issues that drain energy. Tom Sergiovanni told us that successful school leaders keep the important issues of teaching and learning at the center of their work and other issues, such as testing and accountability demands, on the periphery. As mentioned in chapter 4, Shain keeps teaching and learning at the center of her work by defining her job as "the chief advocate for teaching and learning" in the district. She described how her superintendent must divert his attention and energy to political and management issues, such as a recent community controversy about early start times for schools. But her role is not to be distracted by political turmoil and logistical questions but to keep focused on her "North Star": teaching and learning.

Superintendents, too, work to conserve energy by focusing on the central issues and keeping peripheral ones where they belong. In considering time-consuming, state-mandated, compliance paperwork, Choye voiced a perspective that we have heard from many school leaders. State officials "can't possibly read all this stuff." She counsels her staff to "stay focused on how we can help our kids, how we can help our teachers to help our kids." Officials "don't see the faces of these kids who are trying so hard." Canada agreed; he said to conserve energy, it is important to distinguish issues you can control from those you cannot.

School leaders also delegate peripheral tasks in order to protect and conserve their energy for central issues. Fowler was able to find the time and energy to influence state policymaking in four states by trusting important responsibilities to subordinates. "Once I get comfortable with people and I know we share at least a reasonably common value set," he said, "it's very easy for me to take an issue and put in it in their hands and say, 'Run with it.' . . . That has empowered me to be able to do more professionally and also focus on the really difficult [problems] that you get paid for."

Gaither talked about how he keeps energized and enthusiastic by focusing on the central issues of hiring, developing key staff, and building organization capacity rather than "delving into personnel issues" or worrying about "who's suing us, who's mad at us."

Some school leaders, finally, have found new sources of energy in transforming a peripheral issue, such as a state mandate, into a central one, by designing and implementing plans that align the mandate with core values. Thomas told the story about how one of her high school principals and his faculty took a new state mandate that each student have a personal graduation plan and developed a strategy in which every professional in the building, including the administrators, took responsibility for meeting individually with students to develop such a plan. The response from students and parents was "incredibly wonderful." Staff commented, "I hated that the legislature made us do this. But we should have done it all along."

Faith in Ideas

Substantive leadership, according to Sergiovanni, is about ideas. Ideas are the "source of clarity." Ideas can also be a source of mental energy. Phil Schlechty, for example, said, "I get excited about new ideas and different ways of thinking about things. What motivates me is to see a lot of the ideas I'm excited about really work. If you can create a context in which the system encourages growth, people will grow. I have seen it." Fowler agreed. "I think that being involved in a lot of movements—I mean cutting-edge stuff—has always sustained me. I never felt that things were humdrum or monotonous."

In tough situations, Shain turns to ideas to try to help others to make intellectual sense of what is happening. She often finds sense-making frameworks in her reading. One of her favorites is the cycle of committee work: the polite or forming stage; followed by the conflictual or storming state; then the coming-together or norming stage; and, finally, the performing stage. She told us that committees in the storming stage find reassurance in knowing that performing lies ahead.

Thomas, too, looks to books and ideas for new sources of energy. For example, she introduced a book study into principals' groups, with individual members taking turns at presenting and leading discussion. She found that "attention is riveted when their peers are presenting." One consequence is new energy. "We're beginning to have substantive conversations happen on campuses without our having to be present."

A Spiritual Wellspring

More than from these physical, emotional, or mental sources of energy, school leaders develop their energy capacity, recharge their batteries and recover by turning to spiritual sources. From our interviews, it is clear that the wellspring of school leaders' energy is spiritual. Paul Houston, for example, told us, "I don't think it is possible for a person to be at peace without a spiritual base." Loucrecia Collins averred. "There is a higher source of power," she said, "and if you tune into that higher source of strength and energy, you will get through a crisis. There is nothing too big that you can't overcome."

Successful school leaders tend to be spiritual beings. As noted earlier, they must stay connected to their deepest values if they are to persist and withstand the adversity sure to come their way, and for many leaders, those deepest values spring from their spirituality.

As with most people, the spiritual and other values that motivate and drive school leaders have early roots in childhood and family experiences. For a number of the interviewed leaders, the source is religious beliefs engrained in their earliest memories. Alicia Thomas said that among her deepest values is to "meet the needs of other people." She described it as "very aligned with what you learn in Sunday school." In describing his belief in servant leadership, Houston told us, "You need to acknowledge that you are connected and have access to the power beyond us. I am not the center of the universe." Canada said that religious faith can "imbue your moral values in the secular world. . . . People know that you can see that connection even though you never talk about it." Gene Carter also talked about translating religious beliefs into secular values. "I don't define faith in terms of going to church every Sunday, of doing all of those traditional sorts of things and then acting differently on a day-to-day basis," he said. "I have attempted to translate the values I have learned within my church in ways that I feel have the best potential to guide me in living the life I think I should be living. And developing the set of ideals that enable me to treat people as I would want to be treated."

Whatever their source, the effective school leader's values translate into a powerful sense of mission. Dennis Sparks, for example, told us, "Our most compelling purposes come from a moral sense. We have a reason for being." For many, like Maria Goodloe, the mission is a deep belief that the kind of transformation necessary in urban schools to close the achievement gap can be accomplished. Her mission energizes her "because I know that we can do better. It's already been proven." Thomas said that mission becomes a "calling" that, as a source of energy, is the antidote to "burnout." Vince Ferrandino advises principals of the importance of mission in maintaining passion, commitment, and energy. "You need to remind yourself every day of what brought you into education," he suggested.

Energy Management

Transforming Negative to Positive

In our research, we found incredible dynamism, an energy force in the "can do" spirit of school administrators. Successful school leaders harness physical, mental, emotional, and spiritual energy to transform negative situations into positive ones. Herman Gaither does not like to lose, but, he commented, "I always say that the one thing I learned as I went through life was that as soon as an obstacle shows itself, most people start figuring out how they can defend the positions they have taken. I immediately start figuring out how to turn it around."

School leaders like Gaither find energy in—and enjoy the challenge of—turning obstacles into opportunities. Shain described one of these opportunities: "When you get into these situations, you think, 'Is there an opportunity for growth in what appears to be a mess?' And you try and figure out what it is. A particular example was the mandate to 'get the test scores up.' The faculty was concerned that this would turn into test prep instead of instruction. But the best thing that came out of it is a new way of talking to the staff about the link among curriculum, instruction, and assessment. We created a graphic that we put on a mouse pad about the learning cycle and how the parts fit together, and how curriculum and instruction and assessment fit together in a learning environment."

Goodloe found a positive opportunity in an ugly racial incident. As a high school principal, she walked the hallways at lunchtime. One day some students hurled a racial epithet at her while she was on patrol. She was so angry at first that she had to ask an assistant principal to discipline the students. Later, she realized that these students needed training in cultural awareness and respect for differences more than they needed punishment. She then created and team-taught a course on multicultural peer leadership.

Hanson found a positive experience for her school community and herself in the aftermath of Columbine. She described how, like many superintendents who sometimes assume an "evangelistic role," she wrote a letter of comfort to her community: "The letter I wrote said, 'Here's who we are. We believe that security comes through relationships with kids. And when we have wonderful relationships with kids, they'll let us know if there are problems. They will not feel the need to do these things. Our security is in our relationships.' " Hanson did not find the letter difficult to write, she added, because she "truly believes" what she says.

As a school principal, Thomas transformed a negative situation into a positive one and, in the process, unleashed tremendous energy. "And it happened out of adversity. You know the best things do," she commented. As mentioned previously, one afternoon, early in her career, a teacher came to her office and said, "I need to tell you something." The faculty was in crisis. They had met with a local college professor who was supervising intern teachers in the schools and had "united to come back and confront me with all the things they were frustrated about." At first, Thomas felt "sick at heart" about what to do, but the next day at a scheduled faculty meeting, she began a process that she had designed to "get everybody's voice." In small groups, she asked teachers to respond to three questions: What do we have to celebrate? What now needs our attention? What steps do we take next? By the end of the meeting, they began to construct collaboratively an agenda of work for the rest of the year that reenergized and ultimately transformed the school. After the meeting, the feedback indicated that teachers "felt relieved that they were able to dump" their concerns "in an OK" way.

The Power of Personal Choice

An important energy management strategy for school leaders is the personal control over what they choose to do. As Moffett told us, school leaders like to "map out our destinies." Choice can make all the difference in how energized a school leader feels. Some veteran superintendents near or at retirement age, for example, do not feel trapped in their jobs by personal survival needs. No matter how intense the storm, they know that they can always walk away if the pain and stress become intolerable. Gaither remains dynamic and energetic in his 60s. He told us proudly that he could have retired 13 years ago but chose not to because he continues to want to make the Beaufort schools—where he grew up, went to school, and has worked for his whole career—the best that they can be.

Fowler, who recently retired after a career as a superintendent in four districts in four different states, experienced throughout his career the energizing power of personal choice that value-driven leadership provides. He said, "I've never had to worry 'Would they renew my contract?' In fact, I never remember even thinking about that. . . . Once you know that you're doing the right thing, you develop the confidence that you don't have to worry personally. In the final analysis, I would always say, 'Well, if they fire me, I probably shouldn't be with these people anyway, and they may be doing me a favor.' In a sense, they're on the wrong side of the issue and that's what's causing the problem."

Other superintendents, too, talked about how personal work choices energize them. Goodloe chose to lead urban districts because she feels that it's often urban kids who "aren't going to make it." Moffett chose to be a superintendent because she believes it is the position in which one can most quickly and most effectively improve the lives of poor, minority children. Despite the rigors of the superintendency and the fact that the storms she faces can be debilitating, she does not feel trapped, "Even if I decide not to remain a superintendent, I could do something else in the field."

Fully Engaging Through Persistence

To persist over the long haul and be successful, you must maintain and manage your energy by keeping your motivation and determination high and thus stay fully engaged and performing at peak effectiveness. Motivation and determination, in turn, depend in part on your hope. According to Peter Block, hope springs from "a belief in the capacity of the universe. Every human being has the capacity to be good and true." In defining hope during our interview, Sergiovanni distinguished hopefulness from wishfulness: You can wish something to be true without having any hope that it can be accomplished. Hope requires some belief that things can be different. Choye said, "Hope is always looking at the glass as half full." But hope also carries the belief that the rest of the glass can be filled. As Roland Barth told us, "The good people I know who aren't getting beaten down see frequently enough examples of the difference it makes to get up and go to school." The school leaders we interviewed provided hopeful perspectives on their work, as the examples from their practice in this chapter indicate.

As a source of energy, hope is an active state. To stay hopeful, to act on hope, you need persistence, or the ability to "hang in there" despite storms and setbacks. As Sergiovanni said, "Hope is hard work." He also cautioned, "You have to be persistent about something that is important. It needs to be strong enough, I think, to be worth taking chances, taking risks."

Successful school leaders understand the importance of persistence. Hanson said, "You need to have a lot of faith in yourself and a huge amount of tenacity because tenacity makes up for times when things are not working out the way you want, or people are disgruntled, or people don't share your vision of where you're going."

Gaither, too, expressed the value of persistence. "You're not going to get to where you want to go in a year or in two years or three years." He looks at a time frame of five to seven years for major school system reforms. In the early years of a high school reform project in Beaufort, for example, many faculty members resisted becoming involved, perhaps doubting that the district would remain committed or even hoping that the district would not. But when the reform persisted and gathered momentum under the leadership of a dynamic, new high school principal, "the late majority" among the faculty, as Gaither calls them, began to get on board.

Choye has demonstrated a different kind of persistence, "going the extra mile" to strengthen board confidence and trust. A community controversy arose in Scotch Plains when a drama director from a neighboring district refused to direct a Scotch Plains high school show unless he could bring a student to play one of the lead roles. The board initially resisted the plan, feeling that only Scotch Plains students should be cast. When a board member asked Choye whether she had asked the drama director directly, yes or no, whether he would take the job if his student were not in the production, Choye acknowledged that she had only met with the potential drama director in a group of other people and had not asked him directly. The board member, who was unhappy with Choye's answer, reiterated the importance of this information. The next day Choye went to the neighboring district, posed the question, and received a direct no. She said, "I felt it was important that the board knew that I took their comments seriously."

Fueled by hope, persistence demands both mental and emotional energy. As we discussed previously, when you achieve full engagement, you are in the "zone," or what Mihaly Csikszentmihalyi calls the"flow" state, when your mental focus is so concentrated, so persistent, that you feel so motivated that you even lose track of time. Sergiovanni talked about the link between persistence and flow this way: "I think persistence is somewhat related to flow—at least healthy persistence is. And I think everybody experiences it at one time or another. You might have experienced it shooting baskets in the driveway. . . . Three hours may have gone by, and it would seem like 10 minutes because you've entered this state of flow. Persistence and flow are cousins."

Adaptive Distancing

As you will recall from the previous chapter, adaptive distancing enables a leader to manage emotions by finding an "eye in the storm." Hanson described how she practiced this approach in order to gain perspective on her own reactions: "Let's say that I'm in a board meeting, and I have a board member who is annoying, and I feel like I have little control over the situation. I feel my neck getting flushed, and I'm getting so irritated. One of my strategies—and it's a perspective-gaining strategy—is just to step outside myself and go to the balcony and pretend I'm at a play. And now I'm watching myself get riled about some tiny little thing. And it's a perspective setter, because when you watch yourself in the play, it's puny, and it's stupid and it's little petty politics, and it's not important."

Energy Recovery

School administration is a 24/7 profession. Many school leaders spend three or more nights a week at school-related activities—board, PTA, and community meetings; sporting events; school plays; and musical events. And, unlike many other professions with evening commitments, these night responsibilities occur after a full 9- or 10-hour day of work. One of Paul Kelleher's children once remarked that Kelleher had "two jobs—his day job and his night job." Weekends do not bring reliable relief from work stress. School activities occur regularly, and paperwork waits to be completed. Plus, a pile of professional reading is always there to remind you of another responsibility.

To achieve a state of full engagement, you must take the recovery time to replenish physical, emotional, mental, and spiritual energy. Management of energy, including periods of disengagement to renew it, is crucial to resilience.

In our interviews with school leaders, we discovered that they use a range of strategies to take care of themselves and find the support necessary to replenish energy supplies. Canada discussed the importance of friends and family in his personal renewal efforts: "If you don't personally take care of yourself, it can be detrimental," he advised. "In Oregon, I was so committed that I was actually working when I was ill. And the district's attorney, who's actually a very good friend, called my wife to say, 'You know, you really do need to tell Ben to stay at home, because we're all concerned about him. We know that he's committed, but if he's not well, the whole system suffers.' And that was a wake-up call to remind me of something that I've talked to others about, and that is to take care of yourself. . . . We have to really stress the value of being true to the issue about not only knowing yourself but protecting yourself by taking some time off to rethink and to relax and recharge your batteries. Take some time to go to some dinners during the week with your spouse—and you have to commit to it just like I committed to saying I was going to go to school. You have to commit to some time to say, 'I'm sorry, I have a commitment on this evening or this week,' because [otherwise] the spouse does suffer."

In our research and experience, successful school professionals have recovery rituals like those Canada recommends—specific behaviors at specific times that enable them to replenish their energy supplies despite this relentless pace of work demands. Many school leaders build energy recovery into the time between the end of their day job and their evening activity—between approximately 5 and 7 p.m. Some stop whatever they are doing to go home for dinner with their family. Others choose this time of day for regular exercise. One superintendent we know takes an hour nap after the staff has left for the day, before he resumes the rest of his own activities.

Leaders practice a variety of recovery rituals. Some, such as Moffett, go to healing places, like a country retreat in the mountains. Others, such as Shain and Thomas, find recovery strategies in books. Still others, such as Choye, find "head breaks" in scheduling a "down weekend" or in attending a stimulating professional conference outside the school district. Like a number of others, Choye said, "I come back refreshed with a new point of view."

Many leaders find that relationships reenergize them and enable quicker recovery from setbacks. Goodloe, for example, described situations in which she turns to a confidante outside the school system for advice and support. Thomas relied on friends or her staff to help her through a faculty crisis. Both Shain and Hanson described the need to vent with others whom they trust to discover what they really feel and think and then to figure out what to do.

Energy Leadership

To be an effective leader who stimulates positive organizational energy, full engagement, and peak performance, you must manage not only your own emotions but also those of the people whom you lead (Goleman, 1995). The most obvious occasions for emotional and energy leadership are moments of crisis when negative emotions—especially fear and anxiety—can rob an organization of its ability to respond effectively. The school leaders whom we interviewed were keenly aware of this challenge. Gaither, for example, told us, "In moments of crisis, generally I'm smiling. You can't prepare yourself for every crisis, but you can prepare yourself to respond to every crisis. In moments of crisis, you've got to be able to decide 'Where do I go with my energies? What kind of outcome do I want?' "

Hanson talked about the importance of a leader's having the strength to carry people through periods of doubt and uncertainty. She described a time during a bond referendum campaign when, in response to community criticism, her board began to question their design decisions. She could visualize the building and told her board, "We're not going to change the design. It's going to be funded, and it's going to be beautiful." Looking back on her success with this project, Hanson said that "keeping board faith in the project" was essential. She commented, "I think that most superintendents have that quality. But I think you have to have it, because if you flag, if you don't have the confidence . . . it's all over."

The leaders whom we interviewed stimulate positive organizational energy and full engagement by developing the emotional and energy capacity of the people with whom they work. They recognize that their success and the success of the organization depend on this collective capacity. Choye said when new staff members revisit old problems, she resists the reflexive response of defending the old solutions. She must help them find new solutions. "If, in fact, I'm building a strong team because I want to be able to move this wonderful place. . . I must build on the talents of the people I work with," she said.

Like a number of our interviewees, Herman Gaither described his joy in watching people grow. He remembered, for example, one of his current assistants when she was a shy high school student in a geometry class that he taught. Considering her growth over time, he said, "You take satisfaction in that. This is not about Herman. This is about how much you have been able to influence the growth of people, and the growth of people who come to grow in the organization."

Hanson told us that a key to unleashing positive organizational energy is through tapping into people's creativity. She said of her administrative team, for example, "Together our creativity was better than any one person's creativity and that creativity is incredibly motivating and sustaining." In her view, creativity produces energy that becomes a powerful organizational force.

"I modeled creativity," Hanson said, "because there would be times when I would go to a meeting, and I could see there was not anybody in the room who was able to think of some 'out there,' crazy approach. So I would throw some on the table. . . . And I explained to people when I throw an idea on the table, everybody's job around the table is to dissect it, tear it apart, throw it away, and improve it. And their job is to throw ideas on the table, and we'll do the same thing. Hardly anybody could do that at the beginning. I would put an idea on the table, and they'd say, 'OK, we'll do it.' And I'd say, 'No, stop. It's a flawed bad idea, but it's the best I have, so take it.' Eventually people became extremely comfortable with that, and the ideas didn't have personal ownership. But I think it took about three years for us to get to the point where collectively we could throw our ideas on the table."

Summary

To be a successful leader, you must develop your energy capacity and guard against the debilitating effects of ceaseless energy expenditure without adequate recovery periods. Physical energy is the fuel for all other kinds of energy, so you must first take care of yourself through diet, exercise, and sleep. As our research has confirmed, another wellspring of energy is your spiritual values—reconnect with them regularly. Your ability to achieve your best performance also depends on maintaining and expanding your mental energy—keeping focused, getting in the "flow"—and emotional energy—managing your emotions carefully, avoiding the debilitating effects of negative feelings, and building on the powerful consequences of positive feelings. Expanding your energy capacity in these ways will serve to increase your resilience capacity in the face of future storms.

10

FROM PERSONAL RESILIENCE
TO TEAM RESILIENCE

The primary emphasis of this book is on personal resilience, how individual leaders move ahead in the face of adversity. But leaders' personal resilience affects and is affected by the resilience of the organization that they are leading. In other words, for most leaders to be resilient over the long haul, they need a resilient organizational culture to work within. It's tough going it alone on a sustained basis. Roland Barth expressed these sentiments in his interview: "Leaders are starting to recognize that the John Wayne and Joan of Arc rescue model is over with."

When storms strike an organization, the collective resilience of those inside the organization helps determine whether the organization plateaus after the storm at the dysfunctional, survival, recovery, or growth level of functioning. In this chapter, we discuss ways that leaders can help teams within the organization move through tough times to reach the growing phase in the resilience cycle. The term *team* in this context can represent groups as broad as the multicultural citizens of the whole school district or as narrow as the social studies faculty in a high school. Every organization has subcultures with their own levels of team resilience.

Distinctions Between Personal Resilience and Team Resilience

As we discussed in Chapter 1, individual resilience draws most heavily from the field of individual psychology. But as Michael Fullan reminded us, "The individualistic solution [to becoming more resilient] is only half of the solution. The other half of the solution is trying to change the organizational side, the organizational culture."

In our interviews with Fullan, Barth, and Phillip Schlechty, all of them made clear that leaders need to understand the sociology of organizations to lead organizations through tough times. Schlechty said, "My whole life from 1959 until now has been a serious effort to use sociology to make sense of schools and what's going on in the world around schools." He then illustrated the difference between an individual psychology orientation and an organizational sociology orientation. "The Constitution is a sociological document. The Declaration of Independence is a psychological document. The Declaration of Independence says people will sit down and rationally do things. The Constitution says we have to have some roles and relationships established. We have to have power distributed [among subgroups] because individuals are going to behave stupidly at times. So what you do is create systems that make it very difficult for Richard Nixon, as an example, to completely screw up the system."

The sociology of organizations includes an emphasis on the culture of organizations. According to Fullan (2002), "Reculturing is the name of the game. Transforming culture, changing what people in the organization value and how they work together to accomplish it, leads to lasting change" (p. 18). Barth (2002) extends the argument by asserting that a school's culture has more influence on life and learning in the school than the president of the country, the state department of education, or any of the school district's senior administrators. Correspondingly, he contends that culture change is the most difficult and most important job of leaders today.

This difficult job becomes even more difficult in the face of adversity, adversity that apparently is not going to go away anytime soon. Illustrative of the point, over the past few years I (co-author Jerry L. Patterson) have asked thousands of workshop participants a series of questions about changes in education. Specifically, I begin by asking participants to list changes that have affected their professional lives in the last three years. Not surprisingly, participants fill pages of chart paper with topics such as No Child Left Behind (NCLB), state-imposed mandates, fewer resources, increased expectations, school violence, a rise in litigation, decreased parent support, and the list goes on. Next I ask, "Given what you have presented as changes in the recent past, as you look ahead to the next three years, do you think the rate, complexity, and volume of change will decrease, stay about the same, or increase?"

Repeatedly and consistently, people from across the United States and beyond respond with a common refrain. More than 90 percent of the school leaders polled projected that the rate, complexity, and volume of change will increase! And virtually all of the changes that people identified on their lists were changes imposed on them by others. The results of my informal polling vividly captures an important message for leaders: Given the long list of changes that have occurred over the past three years, the next three years will bring even more changes, more adversity, than people have experienced previously. In other words, compared to three years from now, today is the good old days.

If today is the good old days, what can leaders do to position their organizations for tomorrow's adversity? A large part of the answer has been addressed in the first nine chapters of this book—bracing for change starts with the personal resilience of the leader. But it doesn't end there. Team resilience is crucial, too. In this chapter, we make the shift from *I* to *we* as we discuss three dimensions of team resilience (Figure 10.1): team interpretation of adversity, team resilience capacity, and team actions to achieve resilience.

Team Interpretation of Adversity

The first dimension, team interpretation of adversity, looks at how we collectively assess past and current reality and future possibility. Teams, just like individuals, position themselves most effectively for storms in their life when they embrace team characteristics of realistic optimists. Teams that are realistically optimistic

- Accept the realities of organizational life but refuse to regard them as barriers;
- Take responsibility for their team's contribution to the current adversity;
- Accurately assess the risks by striving to have enough data to judge what's really going on;
- Believe in the power of the team to positively influence the future, within the constraints of reality;
- Believe that good things can happen but recognize that it will require a lot of team effort;
- Acknowledge the problems but choose to emphasize the positive possibilities that the team can help create.

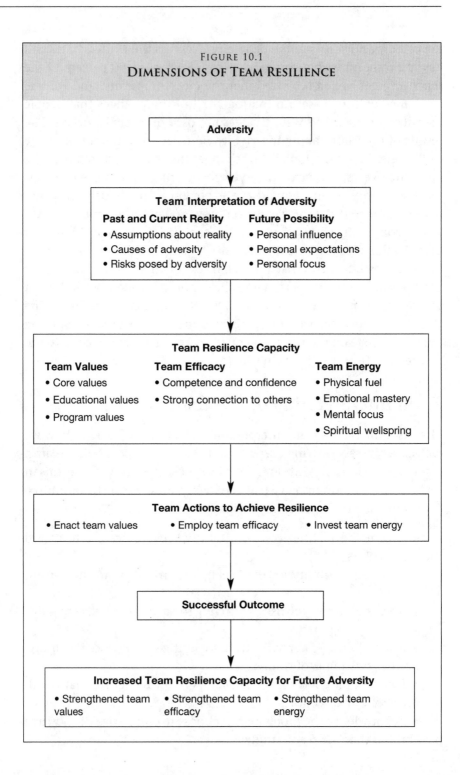

FIGURE 10.1
DIMENSIONS OF TEAM RESILIENCE

Adversity

Team Interpretation of Adversity

Past and Current Reality
- Assumptions about reality
- Causes of adversity
- Risks posed by adversity

Future Possibility
- Personal influence
- Personal expectations
- Personal focus

Team Resilience Capacity

Team Values
- Core values
- Educational values
- Program values

Team Efficacy
- Competence and confidence
- Strong connection to others

Team Energy
- Physical fuel
- Emotional mastery
- Mental focus
- Spiritual wellspring

Team Actions to Achieve Resilience
- Enact team values   • Employ team efficacy   • Invest team energy

Successful Outcome

Increased Team Resilience Capacity for Future Adversity
- Strengthened team values
- Strengthened team efficacy
- Strengthened team energy

For a team to embrace these beliefs authentically, it must be led by an individual with high resilience. The leader sets the tone and tenor when adversity happens. As the independent investigation board concluded in its report on NASA's *Columbia* space shuttle disaster (discussed in chapter 4), "Leaders shape culture. It is their responsibility to change it." During tough times, the pressure on leaders is even greater. Larry Lezotte reflected on leaders with whom he has worked during times of adversity: "When a person tries to grow a set of cultural values," he said, "there is a critical period when the whole culture sits on the shoulders of that leader. I have watched it over and over again that when things change, the [cultural] roots aren't deep enough to hold."

This may seem like a heavy burden to place on the leader's shoulders, yet it is just one of many harsh realities. The challenge becomes, "What are you going to do about it?" Leaders who are realistic optimists accept the conditions imposed by organizational realities, and they work within this perspective of reality to help prepare others, particularly those who also hold leadership roles, not to be shaken when the realities occupy center stage of organizational life. Gerrita Postlewait shared her perspective and expectations for those who work with her on the leadership team: "It is our job to take whatever circumstances come our way and overcome them. I have to fight to have tolerance with people who view themselves as perpetual victims. Every day is another at-bat for us. And nobody bats a thousand. We believe that after a while there is nothing anybody throws over the plate that you and your colleagues can't handle together.

"In our educational system," she added, "we all are here to improve the conditions of children. If someone starts the 'yes, but' replies, my answer is that we as adults are in this system to figure out how to make the conditions over which we have control better. When we are finished venting [about adversity], if we still only see ourselves in this system as victims, then we can't help, and therefore we don't belong in the system."

Postlewait's pointed comments reflect those made by other interviewees. When storms strike, successful organizational cultures stare down the storm. They accept the storm as reality and figure out ways to move through it.

Another strategy that leaders use to glean an accurate interpretation of reality is to surround themselves with others on the leadership team who bring multiple, diverse perspectives to the table. When leaders take the bold step to invite dissenting voices into the conversation, these actions have significant ripple effects throughout the organization's culture. Schlechty talked in his interview about being brought into the central office as the voice of dissent.

"You have to have somebody in charge of messing up the system," he told us. "I learned that from Jay Robinson [Schlechty's former superintendent]. Jay hired me as the special assistant to the superintendent. Jay had a deputy in charge of day-to-day operations and then he had me in charge of messing up the system. I can remember one time when we had a big administrative retreat down at Southern Pines. I called it a 'bare your heart' retreat. The three assistant superintendents were raising hell because I was getting privileges they weren't getting. I didn't have to come in at 8 o'clock. I could take off and do stuff they couldn't do. When people started complaining, Jay leaned back in his chair and said, 'Well, I tell you, I have three good assistant superintendents sitting here. I don't need another good assistant superintendent. In fact, Phil wouldn't be a good one if I made him one. I need someone to come in and help me figure out where the system needs messing up, and it's you folks' job to fix it. And I'll tell you what else. If Phil starts acting like an assistant superintendent, I will fire him.' "

Others whom we interviewed emphasized the need to be surrounded by those who will provide candid feedback about the reality of "what's going on around here," as well as a reality check on the leader's perspective. Linda Hanson illustrated this point: "I can recall my saying to the administrative cabinet, 'I am such a believer in asset building, but I find myself shifting to the deficit model when I talk about [a particular person]. You all have to help me so that I don't stay stuck in the deficit model, because I am really having a hard time with this one.' "

Postlewait also emphasized the importance of encouraging a culture of open dialogue about the realities of what's happening. And it's not just a matter of leaders' announcing an open-door policy. "I realized that an open-door policy might not be the best way to help people manage huge issues," she admitted. "At least it is not enough. They need time to sit down and talk about what is important to them. The system of open dialogue and questioning is what we are trying to do. People [in the culture] should not be embarrassed to say that they need two hours of time to talk about important stuff."

The strategies that are being described here address ways to act out the organizational value of teams being realistically optimistic in their interpretation of past and current reality, as well as believing in the possibility of the future. In the next section, we look at another belief—what we call the "capacity of we."

Team Resilience Capacity

Team resilience capacity is built on three sources of strength: team values, team efficacy, and team energy. Team values reflect the deeply held philosophical beliefs about what matters most in each area of the Personal Values Hierarchy described in Chapter 4. To illustrate the resilience capacity of teams in the area of a team's core values, let's look at the category of shared decision making. Many leaders espouse the value of shared decision making, but, as one leader quipped in a workshop, "My version of shared decision making goes like this: 'Team, I just made a decision, and I would like to share it with you.' " Imagine the impact on team resilience when this value shapes the actions of the leader and, consequently, the other members of the so-called team. When your team faces adverse conditions, what values drive your decisions in response to the adversity?

- Does your team truly believe that the power to make decisions should be extended to the team as a single *we?*
- Does your team believe that the collective expertise of the team usually makes wiser decisions than can be made by the designated leader of the team?
- Does your team value diverse perspectives in trying to make decisions in the face of storms?

In their research on resilient schools, Patterson and colleagues (2002) interviewed a principal in a large urban district who faced chronic adversity. The principal discussed what she learned the hard way about shared decision making: "You can't make a difference as an autocrat, and you can't do it alone," she said. "You have to do it as a team. In the past I have been an addicted enabler. I have taken on the responsibilities that should have been moved to the teachers. So I have had to make a shift from enabler to empowerer. I am still working on it, but there is no alternative" (p. 139).

Team values about shared decision making shape a team's approach to the questions of "Who decides?" and the more important question "Who decides who decides?" In the midst of adversity, teams can't be arguing over whether decisions are going to be made by the team leader, by voting, by consensus, or by unanimous consent. This wasted debate in the heat of battle drains the team's resilience capacity. Teams need to invest time developing and articulating core team values *before* adversity strikes.

A second source of resilience capacity is team efficacy. A team with a strong sense of collective efficacy holds a deeply rooted belief in the group's capability to face any threat that arises with the confidence that the culture will prevail. The team leader, whether the superintendent, principal, or grade-level chairperson, plays a crucial role in creating a social context that enables the team to face storms, achieve successful outcomes, and emerge with increased team efficacy. Henderson and Milstein (1996) have identified several actions that effective school leaders undertake to create a supportive environment that increases collective efficacy. These include offering opportunities for bonding through cooperative activities and creating a sense of belonging to a cause bigger than oneself; providing caring and support through regular, specific feedback, praise, and rewards; and providing opportunities for meaningful participation in decisions.

The research also points to the correlation between feelings of team efficacy and the personal efficacy of principals. Several leaders we interviewed provided firsthand testimony to this point. Lezotte commented, "The successful leaders that I have worked with found it necessary to identify a constituency that they were going to work with. Somebody has got to be their arms and legs. For example, when John Murphy went to Prince George County, Maryland [as superintendent], he essentially took the whole first year to gain the respect of the principals. Of course, every time you make a decision of who you are going to work with, you make enemies at the same time. And the enemies he was making were people at the central office, because they felt like he was dealing directly with the principals. And he was. By the end of the year, the principals were ready to walk through the fire with him."

Ben Canada also remarked on the importance of team efficacy to a leader's sense of personal efficacy: "Your team is as important to your success or failure as anything else you will encounter during your superintendency, and I'm not sure that enough attention is put into the creation and development and then the ability to sustain the team."

Team energy is another variable that directly affects a team's resilience capacity. As we discussed in Chapters 8 and 9, school leaders are energy creators. Their own personal energy directly affects the collective energy of the organization. Resilient leaders recognize this impact and, when storms strike, consciously implement strategies to protect the team members' physical energy, nurture their emotional energy, help center their mental energy, and challenge them to draw on their spiritual energy to sustain them through the storm.

Team Actions to Achieve Resilience

A team's resilience capacity represents the team's potential to make good things happen in the face of a storm. But resilience doesn't result just from strong potential. We argued in Chapter 5 that personal resilience is reflected in the relative alignment among three sets of dynamics:

- What you say you value in relation to what you actually value;
- What you say you do in relation to what you actually do; and
- What you actually do in relation to what you actually value.

Correspondingly, team resilience is influenced significantly by the same set of dynamics applied to the "collective you" as a team (Figure 10.2):

- What your team says it values in relation to what it actually values;
- What your team says it does in relation to what it actually does; and
- What your team actually does in relation to what it actually values.

The health of your team culture is measured by the degree of alignment among each set of dynamics.

A Real-Life Case Study in Team Resilience

The data for the following case study are drawn from two independent reviewers, the National Forum to Accelerate Middle School Reform and

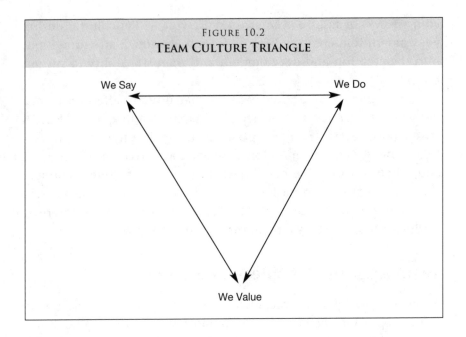

FIGURE 10.2
TEAM CULTURE TRIANGLE

We Say   We Do

We Value

the work of Joan Richardson and the National Staff Development Council (NSDC). Their research focused on the concept of *positive deviants,* those organizations that stand apart from their peers through their performance and ability to align their practices with their core values. Their research culminated in the 2003 publication by NSDC, *From the Inside Out: Learning from the Positive Deviance in Your Organization.*

Freeport Intermediate School in Freeport, Texas, is one of two middle schools in the 13,500-student Brazosport School District. About two-thirds of the students at Freeport Intermediate qualify for the free or reduced-price lunch program. Freeport is a hardworking labor community with a significant number of green card and illegal aliens. Neighboring communities regard the school's neighborhood as unsafe. "It is a tough group to work with," reports a former principal in this part of the state who most recently worked with the Texas Education Agency (see http://schoolstowatch.org/Freeport/fabout.htm for more information). In other words, Freeport Intermediate has its share of adverse conditions. At the same time, the school has worked extremely hard to strengthen the organizational culture by aligning its values with its actions. We will examine its efforts specifically on the core value of student safety.

Freeport Intermediate School staff told independent reviewers that they valued a culture of safety and a goal of ensuring that all students' essential nonacademic needs were met so the students can focus their energy on learning. What the staff said they did to make the value come alive is to "stretch ourselves to the limit to fill in the gaps in students' lives" (National Staff Development Council, 2003, p. 74). The Freeport Intermediate staff also said that providing a safe environment for students to learn is a priority in the allocation of resources. For example, given the number of students who are desperately poor, the school decided to reallocate resources so that a full-time social worker and a full-time nurse could be employed.

In carefully examining the culture of Freeport Intermediate School, external reviewers found that the school's practices were in alignment with what was professed. This was not the case when Principal Clara Sale-Davis first arrived on campus about a decade earlier. "The school was plagued by violence and fear," she said. "We had red bandanas on one side, blue on the other. We had children hating children. We had a dead child from a drive-by shooting. Three of our 8th graders were incarcerated for murder. I thought I had walked into the gates of hell" (see http://www.schoolstowatch.org/Freeport/fresponse.htm for more information).

The external reviewers reported that under the principal's leadership, the school staff worked hard to align their practices with their values about school safety. The school's discipline plan was rewritten and enforced. Breakfast was served at 7 a.m. each day. In the extended-day program, healthy snacks were the first item on the agenda. Adults supervised the physical education locker rooms in the morning so students who were unable to wash at home could shower before classes. Students who needed clean clothes would find them at school, and their dirty clothes were washed at school while the students were in class.

The reviewers found that this emphasis on the safety and nonacademic needs of students reflected the hierarchy of values in the school. As one teacher put it, "You can teach students all you want, but if they don't know that you care about them and their safety, they'll never learn any of it."

This strong alignment between what is professed about a culture of safety and what happens on a daily basis has paid huge dividends. Discipline referrals decreased by 76 percent between September 1995 and

April 2000. One of the reviewers characterized the shift from an environment of violence and fear to one that allowed students to feel safe and supported by noting, "We observed a boy whose clothes and demeanor pronounced him a 'tough guy' gently kneel down and tie the shoes of a young girl with severe disabilities. Apparently unable to speak, she showed her affection by patting him on the head" (see http://www.schoolstowatch.org/freeport/fresponse.htm for more information).

Although the strict discipline policy has helped reduce behavior referrals and engender a sense of safety, teachers and parents say key payoffs are strengthened staff relationships and a belief in their collective efficacy to guide students successfully through the tough times with a relentless focus on high performance. As one reviewer commented, "The change in philosophy has driven Freeport Intermediate School from the bottom of the barrel to the top of the heap on Texas's statewide assessments" (National Staff Development Council, 2003, p. 62). This evidence is vivid testimony to the resilience of the school, students, and community.

The Special Contributions by Teacher Leaders to Team Resilience

This chapter has focused on the importance of team resilience and the leader's role in sustaining it. To emphasize again a point we made in the introduction, we define *leaders* much more broadly than just those sitting in seats of power. Leaders include teachers who have a profound influence on the resilience of team culture. Teacher leaders can serve in formal roles such as department heads, grade-level chairpersons, and members of curriculum task forces.

Informal teacher leaders are those who are recognized by their peers because of their credibility, expertise, or relationship-building skills. Teachers earn credibility when other teachers admire, trust, and respect them for their personal and professional values. As illustrated in the previous section about alignment, teacher leaders consistently align their actions with the needs of the schools' students. Teacher leaders influence team resilience through expertise when their peers recognize their superior teaching skills. The many teacher leaders gaining certification through the National Board for Professional Teaching Standards are illustrative of teacher leader expertise. Finally, teacher leaders positively affect team resilience with their ability to forge relationships—to connect with other teachers as colleagues. Especially during difficult times, teachers turn primarily to one another for support.

Because of these three influences—credibility, expertise, and relationships—teacher leaders make a unique contribution to helping teams use their collective energy to develop team resilience in the face of adversity.

11

Bringing It All Together: The Six Strengths of Resilient Leaders

Throughout this book, we have tried to facilitate a deeper understanding of this thing called resilience. We developed a conceptual framework that outlines three dimensions of resilience. We articulated what we mean by each dimension and why each dimension is important. Then we described in detail how these dimensions come alive in the real world of leaders. We wove the advice and stories of 25 educational leaders into the tapestry of the conceptual framework. Now we bring it all together as we examine the six strengths of resilient leaders (see Figure 11.1).

In this chapter, we show how one resilient leader applies these six qualities as he leads a contentious community effort to redraw district elementary attendance boundaries. We close by describing what happens when any one of the six strengths is absent from the equation.

Newburg Neighborhood Nemesis

The Setting

The Lakeview School District, next to Lake Michigan, is in a conservative, primarily Republican community of about 100,000 residents. The school district is a fast-growing district with a projected enrollment next year of 15,000 students. Population growth has been fueled by several start-up companies in the medical technologies field and by two new high-technology hospitals within a 30-mile radius. The district is governed by a seven-person elected board and led by Superintendent Gwen Pettis. She has been in her position for three years. She enjoys the challenges, and she enjoys the status that her position affords her in the community.

FIGURE 11.1

SIX STRENGTHS OF RESILIENT LEADERS

1. Resilient Leaders Accurately Assess Past and Current Reality. They . . .
   - Expect the world to be filled with disruptions
   - Develop a high tolerance for ambiguity, paradox, and complexity
   - Determine root causes and risks posed by adversity
   - Understand reality from multiple perspectives

2. Resilient Leaders Are Positive About Future Possibilities. They . . .
   - Focus on opportunities, not obstacles
   - Expect that good things can happen despite adversity
   - Exert positive influence to create positive outcomes
   - Maintain a positive perspective for the long-term outcome

3. Resilient Leaders Remain True to Personal Values. They . . .
   - Are clear about what matters most in the hierarchy of values
   - Stay focused on being value-driven, not event-driven
   - Solicit feedback to align values and actions
   - Model for others personal core values

4. Resilient Leaders Maintain a Strong Sense of Personal Efficacy. They . . .
   - Recover quickly from setbacks
   - Achieve and celebrate small wins
   - Maintain confidence in personal competence
   - Sustain a base of caring and support

5. Resilient Leaders Invest Personal Energy Wisely. They . . .
   - Renew physical energy through periodic recovery time
   - Develop emotional empathy and self-awareness
   - Maintain clear mental focus and steady concentration in the face of adversity
   - Invest in spiritual-driven purposes and causes beyond themselves

6. Resilient Leaders Act on the Courage of Personal Convictions. They . . .
   - Are clear about and act on what matters most even when risks are high
   - Act decisively when deepest values are at stake
   - Remain courageous in the face of strong opposition
   - Acknowledge and learn from mistakes by modifying actions to align with values

The Issue

The school district is beginning to feel the school capacity pinch at the elementary school level. With all 14 elementary schools near or above enrollment capacity, the community recently passed a bond referendum to build a new elementary school. Rankin Elementary is scheduled to open next fall. This will mean massive movement of students to balance enrollment across elementary schools. In preparation for these changes, the school board charged the administration with convening a community and staff task force to redraw elementary school boundaries to achieve more equity across schools in terms of race, socioeconomic status, student achievement, and school enrollment.

Dave Schmidt, director for curriculum and instruction, volunteered to chair the task force. He is a lifelong resident of the community who previously served as an elementary principal and baseball coach. Schmidt is an intelligent, empathetic, and well-respected school administrator. He also is savvy about the political undercurrents of power in the community. So when he volunteered to chair the task force, he knew where some of the land mines were buried. One potential explosion was any disruption to the well-entrenched, well-connected families in Newburg Neighborhood. Schmidt had previously observed their feistiness firsthand when they petitioned the school board to hire a Talented and Gifted (TAG) teacher at "their" elementary school, Fennemore Elementary. Although the Newburg Neighborhood students made up about 40 percent of the school's student population, the Newburg Neighborhood parent advocates consumed about 80 percent of the airtime on Fennemore Elementary School issues. So Schmidt wasn't surprised when the parents successfully lobbied the school board to fund this teacher allocation, over the objection of the superintendent and parents of other schools who cried foul.

Another potential land mine was the likelihood that some families in the Newburg Neighborhood would have to go to school with those "other" children who were poor and generally lower-performing compared with most elementary students in the district. Making matters worse, the Newburg children might have to ride a school bus! Such an idea was unprecedented in this affluent, tight-knit community.

Task Force Politics

Even though Schmidt had known that he was in for a challenging stint as chair, he didn't quite know the magnitude of the challenge: six long, conflict-ridden months filled with 42 meetings by the committee trying to come up with a redistricting plan that met the board's criteria for equity. In addition, the committee held 12 emotionally charged community forums to get feedback on the tentative plans. Schmidt had anticipated some of the conflict. The board had directed that the school communities select their own representatives to the task force. Not surprisingly, the loudest, most aggressive voices showed up on the committee. In addition, the church communities were invited to select representatives. The churches that took the initiative to appoint a task force member tended to be those from the more affluent communities, including, of course, the Newburg Neighborhood.

In addition to the loud voices just mentioned, other vocal people on the committee had the self-appointed agenda to make sure that the neighborhoods known to produce the most potential athletes stayed together at the same school.

Schmidt had more trouble than just the political mess. He created some of the mess himself. He made some statements privately to the school board about the petty conduct of some task force members, and his comments got back to the committee members, who in turn confronted Schmidt about his remarks during an already-tense committee meeting. Schmidt acknowledged his mistake, pledging to honor strict confidentiality in the future. Ironically, certain complaining task force members didn't feel compelled to honor the pledge themselves. And they continued a whispering campaign about "You can't trust Schmidt." Schmidt's children and wife became the object of hurtful comments such as "Why doesn't your dad keep his nose out of our school's business? He is just doing this to get attention and get the superintendent's job."

Schmidt's Support Base

Schmidt had a strong base of caring and support from his wife and his parents, who lived in the area. Moreover, he had nurtured a close professional relationship with a mentor superintendent in a nearby district. The superintendent had labored through two redistricting plans previously, so she had some wounds and residual baggage of her own that helped her provide needed counsel and empathy to Schmidt. Schmidt also received both support and unsolicited advice from his golfing buddies. One buddy forecast that this debacle waiting to happen would cost Schmidt a shot at the superintendency, a promotion that Schmidt would welcome at some point in the future.

Schmidt's Motives

Even though Schmidt questioned himself occasionally, deep down he knew why he had volunteered for the leadership role. Throughout his career, he had stayed grounded and clear about his highest priorities educationally. Schmidt wanted all students in the district—and he truly meant *all*—to have an equitable opportunity for a first-class education. He also passionately believed in students experiencing the rich diversity of perspectives, in terms of economics, race, as well as lifestyles, that the community represented. Admittedly, the diversity currently was segregated into vastly disparate neighborhoods. These values kept Schmidt centered. Although there were moments when he thought that he was withering on the inside, he never flinched on the outside. He stood his ground. He believed in himself and he believed in the community. Schmidt felt that when the final board vote was taken, the community and the board could come through this mess in good shape.

Current Status

After too many meetings, a lot of heat, and a few firestorms of protest during the community input at board meetings, Schmidt finally coached the task force to reach a recommendation. On a split vote by the task force, the recommendations included a two-part solution, one short-term and one long-term. In the short run, parents in the schools that would lose students to other elementary schools could keep their children at the neighborhood school if they currently were in the 4th and 5th grades. In other words, these children would be exempt from the decision and could "graduate" from their neighborhood school. Also, the recommendations stated that transfers were voluntary for the next two years. Parents were encouraged to send their children to schools that offered diverse experiences. The district would cover transportation. In addition, the new elementary school would be located in the less affluent section of town. This recommendation was intended to help attract students from other neighborhoods to the newest facility and offer residents in the lower-income neighborhoods more equity in facilities.

The final part of the task force recommendation called for the school board, two years from now, to enact a policy mandating student transfers to achieve equitable conditions that had not been addressed through voluntary measures.

These recommendations were presented to the school board for action on Thursday night. The board finally reached a conclusion at 2:00 a.m. on Friday. Later on Friday a weary Schmidt felt the need to do some personal reflection on this ordeal. He remembered Larry Lezotte's advice in *Resilient School Leaders,* that everybody should go off to their own version of Walden Pond to reflect on what matters most. So Schmidt took his underlined copy of the book and headed to his version of Walden Pond, his hunting cabin up north.

Reflections on the Six Strengths

After settling in and pouring a stout cup of coffee, Schmidt grabbed a yellow legal pad and pencil, opened the book to the page listing the Six Strengths of Resilient Leaders, and started to reflect on how he measured up. He captured the following reflections on his pad.

Resilient Leaders Accurately Assess Past and Current Reality. "I knew this ride was going to be a wild one. . . I just didn't realize how wild. I had seen the Newburg Neighborhood Nemesis in action before, so I was prepared for some of their antics. I remember reading somewhere that your resilience isn't reduced by being surprised. It's when you're surprised that you're surprised. That didn't happen to me.

"Thank goodness for my years as a school principal. I feel like I had a reasonable perspective on the reality about what could potentially happen as the events unfolded. People kept asking me what I thought the final recommendations and vote would be like. And I kept saying, 'I don't know.' And I was comfortable with not knowing because I knew we would give the board assignment our best shot and that's the best I could hope for.

"I have to say, at least to myself here in this cabin, that I can't blame the Newburg Neighborhood for advocating an agenda that put their own children first. They were a pain in the butt for me, but I understand their perspective. I have done that kind of advocating for my own kids, even at the expense of the greater cause sometimes. I guess that is the nature of our wiring as parents.

"All in all, I think I had a pretty good handle on this strength, but I wouldn't have 10 years ago."

Resilient Leaders Are Positive About Future Possibilities. "I'm not so sure about this one. It's mighty tough to stay positive when you are surrounded by negatives. There weren't very many people involved in this who could step back and take a relatively objective look at a positive future. So I did get down on myself at times. Even at my 'downest,' though, I still believed something good could come from the mess. As we chuckled in one task force meeting, 'There's got to be a pony in here somewhere. But it must be buried deep in this smelly stuff.' As chair, I did try to steer us to stay tuned to the charge of more equitable opportunities. And I was OK with the 'yeah, buts,' as long as we got back on track of being value driven. I tried hard to be a positive model, but I know my self-doubts were transparent at times."

Resilient Leaders Remain True to Core Values. "There was never any question in my mind about what matters most to me in this battle. Those children who are disenfranchised from the system deserve the best we can offer. They deserve a shot at quality education. And the children of the movers and shakers need to be exposed to the diversity that our community—indeed, our world—offers. So these were the high-order values that propelled me to stay the course when the going got really rough. Thank goodness I had a couple of trusted task force members who could privately tell me when my actions started to drift away from what matters most. Like the time I lost my cool and told the task force, 'Why don't you guys just go ahead on this project without me? It doesn't seem like you are open to entertaining my perspective on matters.' At the break, Mrs. Henderson called me aside and said that my unplanned and heated comments could get in the way of future progress: 'You don't want to jeopardize the big picture.' I had to force myself to keep my eyes on the long-term prize (an equitable solution) and returned after the break with an apology for my outburst. Then I got back on track of chairing the meeting, not proselytizing to others.

"One of the highest compliments that I received was when a task force member said to the group as we neared the end of our endless meetings, 'It's pretty clear what Mr. Schmidt cares about. It is evident in his leadership on this issue. He has consistently modeled what he stands for.' Boy, I needed that."

Resilient Leaders Maintain a Strong Sense of Personal Efficacy. "I have a long track record of doing a pretty good job in this district, if you ignore two losing seasons as baseball coach. I knew I was up to the task. If I was a rookie around here, I wouldn't have been so self-assured. But I have been knocked down before and bounced back. And when you put this issue next to the issue of losing my brother in a car accident and my mom's bout with cancer, this task force challenge pales in comparison. But I didn't do a very good job of reminding myself to celebrate the small wins along the way. When the task force finally adopted a set of ground rules about how we would conduct business, that was a breakthrough and was due in large part to my skills in facilitating the group. But I lost sight of this and was disappointed at the end of the meeting because I couldn't get them to accomplish more. Oh, well. Next time.

"Thank goodness for my family and colleagues through all of this. When I would come dragging home after a five-hour task force meeting, Bobbi would still be awake and had soft music playing and a baked treat to boost my spirits. Plus, she is just a great listener. It's a good thing, because I wore her out 'processing' all of the ins and outs of the meeting. The biggest boost of all is when she secretly arranged to whisk me away for a long weekend escape to the mountains. And Martha Jayne, colleague superintendent, was invaluable in extending kind words of support. But it was more than that. She offered insights from her own experiences with redistricting that helped me put things in better perspective. I must say, with all of the angst that this assignment has brought me, I feel stronger to take on another difficult task in the future."

Resilient Leaders Invest Personal Energy Wisely. "I need to give myself a failing grade on the whole business of wisely investing my physical energy. I plowed ahead week after week and didn't give my body time to recover. Except for the trip to the mountains, there were no breaks in the action. And this took its toll on me. I am exhausted right now and have been for about a month. I know my exhaustion limited my leadership effectiveness in the closing weeks of our work.

"At the same time, I can give myself rather high marks for staying mentally focused on the task at hand. I refused to be taken off track. I thought about our task force work all of the time. Probably I let the mental focus get in the way of what Goleman calls my emotional intelligence. I tried to have empathy for the Newburg Neighborhood Nemesis, but I didn't have much fuel in my tank for that. I also didn't have much in reserve for clearly assessing my own emotional self-awareness. I'll do better with that next time.

"The source of energy that I always knew I could count on was my religious beliefs. As a strong Catholic, I turned to my deep faith as a source of energy when things got messy. The bottom-line purpose of this task force, in my humble opinion, was creating a better life for others."

Resilient Leaders Act on the Courage of Personal Convictions. "I'll say this: It does take a lot of courage to expose yourself to public criticism, even ridicule. But I got through it intact. Courage, it seems, is acting on your convictions. As Paul Houston says in *Resilient School Leaders,* without actions all you have are assertions. I think I did more than just assert my beliefs. On balance, I acted on my values, and I take pride in it. I sure made some mistakes along the way, too. Like the time I lost it with the task force and was close to quitting. Thank goodness for Mrs. Henderson's comments to get me back on track.

"As I reflect on my own resilience through this ordeal, I guess I held up OK. I'm ready to tackle something else that is worth fighting for. But I don't guess I will be fighting for the superintendency in this district. Because the board rejected our task force recommendations on a 4–3 vote, and because they blamed me for not having adequately considered the community voices who were objecting to the plan, I had better shift my superintendent aspirations elsewhere. But you know what? I guess this is the greatest testimony to my resilience. I am at peace with the outcome. I gave it my best effort consistent with what I value most. And I refuse to be judged or to judge myself by the outcome of a vote. Let me be judged by what I stand for."

Closing

The preceding scenario illustrates how Dave Schmidt demonstrated the six strengths of resilient leaders as he led a task force effort in his school district. Collectively, the six strengths form a strong foundation for moving ahead in the face of adversity. Notice what happens, however, when any one of the six strengths is absent from the total equation.

Without the ability to *accurately assess past and current reality,* you have an inadequate picture of "what is really going on around here."

As we discussed in earlier chapters, unrealistic pessimists deny reality, and unrealistic optimists treat reality as incidental to the purpose. Either way, without an accurate determination of risks and causes and without a mind-set that disruptions will happen, resilience is negatively affected. You get blindsided by a reality you weren't anticipating. Schmidt realized this when he observed that he wouldn't have been as resilient in this category 10 years ago. But, as he commented to a golfing buddy during the thick of the Newburg Neighborhood Nemesis, "I don't think about how I am going to deal with reality. I think about making reality deal with me."

Without the ability to *be positive about future possibilities,* you get caught in the trap of seeing the glass half-full or, worse, half-empty. Imagine what would have happened if Schmidt had allowed task force deliberations to dwell on the problems. And there were plenty of problems. If you let your own resilience account become drained by seeing only problems ahead, you in turn negatively affect the resilience of those you are leading. The cumulative impact of seeing only problems creates a sense of hopelessness, a belief that nothing good can happen.

If you don't *remain true to core values,* you have no center. If Schmidt responded to the redistricting challenge without a clear, comprehensive picture of what he and the task force stood for, he would have ended up responding in the typical event-driven pattern that leaders sometimes get trapped into. Once in this trap, you react to criticism by being defensive of your position. You react to the winds of politics by going with the events that will appease the politics of the moment. Without a values-based focus, you don't have anything to offer about what you *do* stand for. You waste resilience points lamenting the negatives when you could be conserving resilience points by staying true to your core values. Over time, a leader without a clear sense of personal values will wake up one day to an empty resilience account.

If you're not *maintaining a strong base of personal efficacy,* you create self-doubt, which becomes a self-fulfilling prophecy. When you doubt your competence and confidence, you expend resilience points worrying about your inadequacies. As you worry, you exacerbate your downward trajectory of resilience. You see your mistakes; you don't see your small wins. You see setbacks as failures, not as natural blips on the path to growth. Leaders who lack personal efficacy often retreat into themselves, shutting out any attempts by others to offer caring and support. Without caring and support, they feel even more alone and less efficacious. The pattern leads to a depleted resilience account.

If you don't have the habit of *investing personal energy wisely,* you sap the fuel supply that can sustain you through tough times. You often feel compelled to push ahead, using up physical energy at a pace that can't be sustained over the long haul. Without recovery, you exhaust your physical energy, and exhaustion is not conducive to effective leadership. Also, emotional energy has a tendency to be drained and not replenished during adversity. When Schmidt lost his temper with the task force and said things that he regretted later, he attributed this "lack of control" in large part to being emotionally drained. Such a condition makes it harder to have emotional empathy for others because your scarce emotional resilience points are being consumed to protect your own emotional state. Similarly, a lack of clear mental focus can drain your resilience. If you can't stay tuned in to the task, energy is wasted, and resilience is siphoned off. Finally, the absence of an anchor in causes beyond yourself negatively affects resilience. Whether in the form of formal religious doctrine or more general spiritual core values, your spiritual base is bedrock for you to sustain your resilience in the long run. Absent the base, personal resilience suffers.

Without the leadership quality of *acting on the courage of your convictions,* strength is not possible. We emphasized throughout this book that a potential strength can't become an actual strength without action consistent with your values. If you are unclear on your deepest values, you have nothing solid to act on. Without convictions, you lose courage to take strong stands in the face of opposition. And when you don't have a pattern of acting consistent with your values, you lose your integrity and your authenticity. Who are you if your conduct is not clearly tied to what you stand for? It becomes even more difficult to be decisive and to acknowledge mistakes when a pattern of personal convictions hasn't been enacted to reinforce to yourself and others what matters most. Depleted resilience is the outcome.

As we have learned from our research and from the rich perspectives of the 25 educational leaders whom we interviewed for this book, each of the six strengths is critical for helping you move ahead in the face of adversity. Together they interact with such powerful force that you can have confidence that you will weather the inevitable storms. Moreover, you will recover and head on an upward trajectory in your journey to the growth phase of resilience. As Paul Houston concluded, "When it comes to resilience, almost all of us have a whole lot more latent capacity than we are ever called upon to use. The fuel tank is full, but we are just not asked to drive very far." We hope this book gives you added fuel, added strength, for your journey amid life's storms.

APPENDIX

THE EDUCATION
LEADERS WE INTERVIEWED

Roland Barth is a consultant to schools, other educational agencies, foundations, and businesses in the United States and abroad. He served as a public school teacher and principal for 15 years in Massachusetts, Connecticut, and California. While on the faculty at Harvard University for 13 years, he served as founding director of the Principals' Center and of the International Network of Principals' Centers, as well as senior lecturer. Barth is the author of many articles and six books, including *Lessons Learned, Cruising Rules, Improving Schools from Within, Run School Run,* and *Open Education and the American School.*

Peter Block is an author and consultant. His work is about empowerment, stewardship, chosen accountability, and the restoration of community. He is the author of several best-selling books: *Flawless Consulting, Stewardship, The Empowered Manager,* and *The Answer to How Is Yes.* The books are about ways to create workplaces and communities that work for all. The focus is to bring change into the world through invitation and connectedness rather than through mandate and force. He is a partner in Designed Learning, which offers workshops designed by Block to build the skills outlined in his books.

Benjamin O. Canada is currently associate executive director, District Services, Texas Association of School Boards. In his 35 years in education, he was superintendent in Portland, Oregon; Atlanta, Georgia; and Jackson, Mississippi. He also served as a special education teacher and in several other administrative roles. Canada has served on numerous boards, including the Harvard Urban Superintendents Advisory Board and the Danforth Forum for the American School Superintendent. He is the recipient of numerous awards, including an honorary doctorate from Lewis & Clark College, Portland, Oregon. Canada also served as president of the American Association of School Administrators (AASA) during 2000–2001. He was the first African American elected to the Executive Committee of AASA and the only African American to be president. Canada is married to his 1st grade sweetheart, and they have two adult daughters.

Gene R. Carter is Executive Director and CEO of the Association for Supervision and Curriculum Development (ASCD). He is a veteran educator with experience as a private and public school teacher, public school administrator, superintendent of schools, and university professor. Before joining ASCD, Dr. Carter served for nine years as the superintendent of schools in Norfolk, Virginia, where he succeeded in reducing the dropout rate, built a partnership program with the private sector, implemented a district-wide school improvement program, established an early education center for three-year olds and their parents, and implemented a regional scholarship foundation for public school students. Dr. Carter serves on the board of directors of a number of corporations and non-profit organizations, and has written numerous articles and book chapters concentrating on educational issues and topics. He is the coauthor of *The American School Superintendent: Leading in an Age of Pressure.*

Carol Choye is currently in her 12th year as superintendent in the Scotch Plains–Fanwood, New Jersey, schools. She as also served as superintendent in Princeton, New Jersey, and as a teacher and administrator in San Francisco. Choye has worked professionally with numerous organizations including Teachers College, Columbia University, the Danforth Foundation for the American School Superintendent, and the Seton Hall Superintendent's Initiative. She was selected by the New Jersey Association of School Administrators as the New Jersey Superintendent of the Year in 1998. She subsequently was selected by the American Association of School Administrators (AASA) as one of four finalists for National Superintendent of the Year.

Loucrecia Collins is an assistant professor in the Educational Leadership Department, University of Alabama at Birmingham. She provides support through instruction and mentoring to aspiring school leaders in the master's and doctoral programs for her department. Her high-energy, interactive classes focus on bringing reality to supervision and organizational theory. A veteran educator, she has been recognized as an award winning teacher in Mississippi, principal in Alaska, and professor. Collins is the author of several articles in the area of conflict resolution and is coauthor of a book on resilience, *Bouncing Back: How Schools Move Ahead in the Face of Adversity.*

Vincent L. Ferrandino is the executive director of the National Association of Elementary School Principals (NAESP). Ferrandino previously served as executive director and CEO of the New England Association of Schools and Colleges and as Commissioner of Education in Connecticut. Prior to these assignments, he held positions in public schools as a teacher, assistant principal, principal, and superintendent. He has served as president of the Association for the Advancement of International Education and as chair of the Board of Governors for the U.S. Department of Education's Regional Laboratory at Brown University. He has received the Distinguished Fellow Award from Phi Delta Kappa.

Charles Fowler, president of School Leadership, LLC, retired as superintendent of schools in Hewlett, New York, in June 2004. In his 35 years as a superintendent, Fowler served in Nassau County, New York; Sarasota County, Florida; Fairfield, Connecticut; and DeKalb, Illinois. He has received many honors from national and international scholarly and service organizations. In 1989, he was awarded the Medal of Honor by Surgeon General C. Everett Koop for his work in support of schoolchildren with AIDS. Fowler is the author of more than 50 books, monographs and articles. He and his wife, Yolanda, have three married children and four grandchildren.

Michael Fullan is the former dean of the Ontario Institute for Studies in Education of the University of Toronto. Recognized as an international authority on educational reform, Fullan is engaged in training, consulting, and evaluating change projects around the world. His ideas for managing change are used in many countries, and his books have been published in many languages. In April 2004, he was appointed special adviser to the premier and minister of education in Ontario. Among his widely acclaimed books are the *What's Worth Fighting For* trilogy (with Andy Hargreaves), *The New Meaning of Educational Change,* and *The Moral Imperative of School Leadership.*

Herman K. Gaither is currently superintendent in Beaufort County School District, South Carolina. He has spent his entire 44-year career in Beaufort, where he has also served as teacher, coach, curriculum specialist, director of finance, and deputy superintendent. During Gaither's tenure as superintendent, Beaufort schools have won national recognition for educational reform efforts such as pioneering technology programs. Among his awards, Gaither is the recipient of the Consortium for School Networking (CoSN) award and the 2002 Withrow Education Outstanding Achievement Award. Gaither and his wife, Romona, have one child, who is himself a school administrator, and two grandchildren.

Maria L. Goodloe is superintendent of schools in Charleston, South Carolina. She has also served as assistant superintendent in Corpus Christi, Texas, as well as in several administrative and teaching positions in Colorado. A recipient of numerous awards, Goodloe received the Alumni Achievement Award from the University of Nebraska at Lincoln in May 2000. She is also a 2003 graduate of the Broad Center for Superintendents, a national training program for identifying, preparing, and supporting successful school district CEOs.

Linda Hanson is the retired superintendent of Township High School District 113 in Highland Park, Illinois. She has taught public school from kindergarten through high school and has served as an elementary and high school principal. She is currently the president of School Exec Connect, a school executive search firm. She has received many awards, including the Illinois Governor's Award for contributions to art education, Outstanding Administrator of the Year for her work with student assistance programs, and the Illinois Crossroads Council Woman of Achievement award. Her doctorate is from Northern Illinois University. She is married to a symphony conductor and has three children, all of whom have given her insightful perspectives into schooling.

Paul Houston has served as executive director of the American Association of School Administrators since 1994. He previously held positions as a teacher and administrator in North Carolina, New Jersey, and Alabama. He has been a superintendent of schools in New Jersey, Arizona, and California. Houston has served as a consultant and speaker throughout the United States and overseas, and he has published more than 100 articles in professional journals. Houston coauthored the books *Exploding the Myths, The Board-Savvy Superintendent, Articles of Faith and Hope for Public Education,* and *Outlook and Perspectives on American Education.*

Larry Lezotte is a pre-eminent spokesperson for continuous school improvement based on effective schools research. As a consultant, he designs training programs not only to inspire schools and districts to adopt the "learning for all" mission, but also to give them the information and tools that they need to plan and implement continuous school improvement. His early research, with colleagues Ron Edmonds and Wilbur Brookover, identified the characteristics of effective schools—schools where all students learn. In addition to his consulting activities, Lezotte has written widely on continuous school improvement. His writings include *The Correlate Book* series, a collection of monographs on the Correlates of Effective Schools.

Jim Loehr is chairman, CEO, and cofounder of LGE Performance Systems, a training company that specializes in helping business executives, elite law enforcement teams, medical professionals, and professional athletes achieve full engagement in high-stress environments. LGE's training system reflects Loehr's conviction that managing energy, not time, is the key to sustained high performance. Loehr has worked with hundreds of world-class athletes, including golfer Mark O'Meara, tennis player Monica Seles, and Olympic gold medal speed skater Dan Jansen. He has authored 13 books, including his most recent, coauthored with Tony Schwartz, *The Power of Full Engagement* (2003).

Josephine Moffett is the superintendent in Greenburgh, New York, Central 7 School District. She also served as superintendent in Freeport, New York, and Greenburgh–North Castle, New York. Her prior administrative positions included directorships in pupil personnel services and special education. Among her accomplishments, she initiated a unique, cross-district magnet academy on a college academy and significantly increased grant funding. She and her husband, Larry, live in Riverdale, New York.

Rubén Olivárez is superintendent of the San Antonio Independent School District. He began his career as an elementary teacher and has served in many teaching and administrative positions throughout Texas. He was a professor and director of teacher education at the University of Texas at Austin, a principal and executive director in the Fort Worth Independent School District, an executive director in the Austin School Independent School District, and associate commissioner and deputy commissioner with the Texas Education Agency. Olivárez joined the Dallas Independent School District in 1996 as an area superintendent and was named associate superintendent one year later.

Gerrita Postlewait has served as superintendent of the Horry County, South Carolina, Schools since 1996. Because of her strong leadership, Horry County Schools has become one of the fastest-improving and strongest-performing school districts in the state. Postlewait has served in a variety of educational roles in her career, including elementary, middle, high school and university teacher; principal; special education director; associate superintendent for learning services; and deputy superintendent.

Phillip Schlechty is the founder and CEO of the Schlechty Center for Leadership in School Reform. Under his guidance, the staff of the Schlechty Center conducts seminars and provides training programs and workshops for superintendents, principals, teachers, school board members, and parent groups. He has taught and held administrative positions in public schools as well at the university level. He has written numerous books and articles, the most recent of which are *Inventing Better Schools, Shaking Up the School House, Working on the Work,* and *Creating Great Schools: Six Critical Systems at the Heart of Educational Innovation* (forthcoming 2005).

Charles Schwahn has made his professional life a study of leadership, change, and future-focused planning. For the past 25 years, he has worked with businesses and schools throughout North America providing consultation on those topics. Schwahn's work is based on his study of leadership and his successful eight-year experience as superintendent of the Eagle County School District in Colorado. He is the coauthor of *Total Leaders,* a best-selling book published by AASA, and *Making Change Happen.*

Thomas J. Sergiovanni is Lillian Radford Professor of Education and Administration at Trinity University, San Antonio. Prior to Trinity, he was professor of educational administration and supervision at the University of Illinois at Urbana-Champaign. Sergiovanni serves on the editorial boards of the *Journal of Personnel Evaluation in Education* and *Catholic Education: A Journal of Inquiry and Practice.* Among his publications are *Moral Leadership: Getting to the Heart of School Improvement* (1992); *Building Community in Schools* (1994); *Leadership for the School House: How Is It Different? Why Is It Important?* (1996); *The Lifeworld of Leadership: Creating Culture, Community, and Personal Meaning in Our Schools* (2000); *The Principalship: A Reflective Practice Perspective* (2001); *Leadership: What's in It for Schools?* (2001); *Supervision: A Redefinition* (2002); and *Strengthening the Heartbeat: Leading and Learning Together in Schools* (2005).

Lynne Shain, assistant superintendent for curriculum and professional development, Westport Public Schools, directs the coordination, articulation, and integration of the K–12 curriculum. Shain coordinates district-wide staff development programs; supervises the Westport Curriculum Center and its personnel; and directs grant management, the ESOL Program, Gifted Program, and the implementation of the Strategic Technology Plan. Prior to her present position, she directed the Westport Teachers' Center, managing existing grants and applying for new ones. She was a teacher of social studies and history for more than 20 years in schools in Washington, D.C.; Rye, New York; New York City; and Westport, Connecticut.

Dennis Sparks has been executive director of the 10,000-member National Staff Development Council (NSDC) since 1984. He is author of *Leading for Results: Transforming Teaching, Learning, and Relationships in Schools; Designing Powerful Professional Development for Teachers and Principals;* and *Conversations that Matter;* and coauthor with Stephanie Hirsh of *Learning to Lead, Leading to Learn: A New Vision for Staff Development.* Sparks's column appears each month in the newsletter *Results,* a publication of the National Staff Development Council. His interviews with leading educational thinkers appear in *JSD,* a quarterly magazine published by NSDC.

Alicia Thomas is associate superintendent for instruction in the North East Schools in San Antonio. Among her other roles, she has served as a teacher, assistant principal, and elementary principal. As an elementary principal, Thomas led one of the first schools in the nation to embrace Ernest Boyer's Basic School principles. She developed a strong relationship with Boyer and the Carnegie Foundation for the Advancement of Teaching, where she served as a mentor for other Basic School administrators. Among her numerous awards, she has won the prestigious Harold W. McGraw, Jr., Prize in Education.

Dan Wertz is superintendent emeritus of the 4,000-student suburban Okemos Michigan School District, after having been the superintendent for 23 years. Prior to serving as superintendent, he was a middle school science teacher; director of instruction at the International School in Bangkok, Thailand; and an assistant superintendent in the Columbus, Indiana, school district. Wertz has conducted research on resilient superintendents in Michigan. Resilient behavior articles by Wertz have been published in *News-Link,* a publication for school leaders worldwide; the *American School Board Journal;* the *American Association of School Administrators* magazine; as well as a Phi Delta Kappa Fastback, *Resilient Superintendents.*

BIBLIOGRAPHY

Ackerman, R. H. (2002). *The wounded leader: How real leadership emerges in times of crisis.* San Francisco: Jossey-Bass.

Ackerman, R. H., & Maslin-Ostrowski, P. (2004). The wounded leader. *Educational Leadership, 61*(7), 28–32.

Aspinwall, L. G., & Staudinger, U. M. (2003). A psychology of human strengths: Some central issues of an emerging field. In L. G. Aspinwall & U. M. Staudinger (Eds.), *A psychology of human strengths: Fundamental questions and future directions for a positive psychology* (pp. 9–22). San Francisco: Berrett-Koehler.

Badaracco, J. L., Jr. (1997). *Defining moments: When managers must choose between right and right.* Boston: Harvard Business School Press.

Bagozzi, R. P. (2003). Positive and negative emotions in organizations. In K. S. Cameron, J. E. Dutton, & R. E. Quinn (Eds.), *Positive organizational scholarship: Foundations in a new discipline* (pp. 176–193). San Francisco: Berrett-Koehler.

Baker, W., Cross, R., & Wooten, M. (2003). Positive organizational network analysis and energizing relationships. In K. S. Cameron, J. E. Dutton, & R. E. Quinn (Eds.), *Positive organizational scholarship: Foundations in a new discipline* (pp. 328–342). San Francisco: Berrett-Koehler.

Baltes, P. B., & Freund, A. M. (2003). Human strengths as the orchestrations of wisdom and selective optimization with compensation. In L. G. Aspinwall & U. M. Staudinger (Eds.), *A psychology of human strengths: Fundamental questions and future directions for a positive psychology* (pp. 23–35). San Francisco: Berrett-Koehler.

Bandura, A. (1995). *Self-efficacy in changing societies.* New York: Cambridge University Press.

Bandura, A. (1997). *Self-efficacy: The exercise of control.* New York: W. H. Freeman.

Barth, R. (2002). The culture builder. *Educational Leadership, 59*(10), 6–11.

Benard, B. (2004). *Resiliency: What we have learned.* San Francisco: WestEd.

Berscheid, E. (2003). The human's greatest strength: Other humans. In L. G. Aspinwall & U. M. Staudinger (Eds.), *A psychology of human strengths: Fundamental questions and future directions for a positive psychology* (pp. 37–47). San Francisco: Berrett-Koehler.

Buchanan, G. M., & Seligman, M. E. P. (1995). *Explanatory style.* Hillsdale, NJ: Erlbaum.

Cameron, K. S., Dutton, J. E., & Quinn, R. E. (Eds.). (2003). Foundations of positive organizational scholarship. In K. S. Cameron, J. E. Dutton, & R. E. Quinn (Eds.), *Positive organizational scholarship: Foundations of a new discipline* (pp. 3–13). San Francisco: Berrett-Koehler.

Cantor, N. (2003). Constructive cognition, personal goals, and the social embedding of personality. In L. G. Aspinwall & U. M. Staudinger (Eds.), *A psychology of human strengths: Fundamental questions and future directions for a positive psychology* (pp. 49–60). San Francisco: Berrett-Koehler.

Caprara, G. V., & Cervone, D. (2003). A conception of personality for a psychology of human strengths: Personality as an agentic, self-regulating system. In L. G. Aspinwall & U. M. Staudinger (Eds.), *A psychology of human strengths: Fundamental questions and future directions for a positive psychology* (pp. 61–74): San Francisco: Berrett-Koehler.

Carter, S. C. (2001). *No excuses: Lessons from 21 high-performing, high-poverty schools.* Washington, D.C.: Heritage Foundation.

Carver, C. S., & Scheier, M. F. (2003). Three human strengths. In L. G. Aspinwall & U. M. Staudinger (Eds.), *A psychology of human strengths: Fundamental questions and future directions for a positive psychology* (pp. 87–102). San Francisco: Berrett-Koehler.

Dutton, J. E., & Heaphy, E. D. (2003). The power of high-quality connections. In K. S. Cameron, J. E. Dutton, & R. E. Quinn (Eds.), *Positive organizational scholarship: Foundations of a new discipline* (pp. 263–278). San Francisco: Berrett-Koehler.

Eisenberg, N., & Wang, V. O. (2003). Toward a positive psychology: Social developmental and cultural contributions. In L. G. Aspinwall & U. M. Staudinger (Eds.), *A psychology of human strengths: Fundamental questions and future directions for a positive psychology* (pp. 117–129). San Francisco: Berrett-Koehler.

Fernández-Ballesteros, R. (2003). Light and dark in the psychology of human strengths: The example of psychogerontology. In L. G. Aspinwall & U. M. Staudinger (Eds.), *A psychology of human strengths: Fundamental questions and future directions for a positive psychology* (pp. 131–147). San Francisco: Berrett-Koehler.

Fredrickson, B. L. (2003). Positive emotions and upward spirals in organizations. In K. S. Cameron, J. E. Dutton, & R. E. Quinn (Eds.), *Positive organizational scholarship: Foundations of a new discipline* (pp. 163–175). San Francisco: Berrett-Koehler.

Fullan, M. (2001). *The new meaning of educational change* (3rd ed.). New York: Teachers College Press.

Fullan, M. (2002). The change leader. *Educational Leadership, 58*(9), 6–10.

Gibbons, F., Eggleston, T., & Benthin, A. (1997). Cognitive reactions to smoking relapse. *Journal of Personality and Social Psychology, 72,* 184–195.

Goleman, D. (1995). *Emotional intelligence.* New York: Bantam Books.

Goleman, D. (2000). *Leadership that gets results.* Boston: Harvard Business Review.

Grotberg, E. (1995). *A guide to promoting resilience in children: Strengthening the human spirit.* The Hague, The Netherlands: Bernard van Leer Foundation.

Heifetz, R. A., & Linsky, M. (2002). *Leadership on the line: Staying alive through the dangers of leading.* Boston: Harvard Business School Press.

Heifetz, R. A., & Linsky, M. (2004). When leadership spells danger: Leading meaningful change in education takes courage, commitment, and political savvy. *Educational Leadership, 61*(7), 33–37.

Henderson, N., & Milstein, M. (1996). *Resiliency in schools: Making it happen for students and educators.* Thousand Oaks, CA: Corwin.

Lencioni, P. M. (2002). Make your values mean something. *Harvard Business Review, 80*(7), 113–117.

Loehr, J., & Schwartz, T. (2003). *The power of full engagement: Managing energy, not time, is the key to high performance and personal renewal.* New York: Free Press.

Luthans, F. (2002). Positive organizational behavior: Developing and managing psychological strengths for performance improvement. *Academy of Management Executives, 16,* 57–75.

Maddux, J. E. (1995). *Self-efficacy, adaptation, and adjustment: Theory, research, and application.* New York: Plenum.

Maddux, J. E. (2002). Self-efficacy: The power of believing you can. In C. R. Snyder & Shane J. Lopez (Eds.), *Handbook of positive psychology* (pp. 277–287). New York: Oxford University Press.

Masten, A. S. (2001). Ordinary magic: Resilience process in development. *American Psychologist, 56*(3), 227–238.

Nansook, P., & Peterson, C. M. (2003). Virtues and organizations. In K. S. Cameron, J. E. Dutton, & R. E. Quinn (Eds.), *Positive organizational scholarship: Foundations of a new discipline* (pp. 33–47). San Francisco: Berrett-Koehler.

National Staff Development Council. (2003). *From the inside out: Learning from the positive deviance in your organization.* Oxford, OH: Author.

Patterson, J. (1997). *Coming clean about organizational change.* Arlington, VA: American Association of School Administrators.

Patterson, J. (2000). *The anguish of leadership.* Arlington, VA: American Association of School Administrators.

Patterson, J. (2003). *Coming even cleaner about organizational change.* Lanham, MD: Scarecrow Education.

Patterson, J., & Patterson, J. (2001). Resilience in the face of imposed changes. *Principal Leadership, 1*(6), 50–55.

Patterson, J., Patterson, J., & Collins, L. (2002). *Bouncing back! How your school can succeed in the face of adversity.* Larchmont, NY: Eye on Education.

Pearsall, P. (2003). *The Beethoven factor: The new positive psychology of hardiness, happiness, healing and hope.* Charlottesville, VA: Hampton Roads.

Peterson, C. (2000). The future of optimism. *American Psychologist, 55*(1), 44–55.

Peterson, C. M., & Seligman, M. E. P. (2003). Positive organizational studies: Lessons from positive psychology. In K. S. Cameron, J. E. Dutton, & R. E. Quinn (Eds.), *Positive organizational scholarship: Foundations of a new discipline* (pp. 14–27). San Francisco: Berrett-Koehler.

Reivich, K., & Shatte, A. (2002). *The resilience factor: Seven essential skills for overcoming life's inevitable obstacles.* New York: Broadway Books.

Richardson, J. (2003). *From the inside out: Learning from the positive deviance in your organization.* Oxford, OH: National Staff Development Council.

Scheier, M. F., & Carver, C. S. (1992). Effects of optimism on psychological and physical well-being: Theoretical overview and empirical update. *Cognitive Therapy and Research, 16,* 201–228.

Schlechty Center for Leadership in School Reform (2005). *Our Philosophy.* Retrieved May 17, 2005 from http://www.schlechtycenter.org/psc/philosophy.asp.

Schneider, S. L. (2001). In search of realistic optimism: Meaning, knowledge, and warm fuzziness. *American Psychological Association, 56*(3), 250–263.

Schulman, P. (1999). Applying learned optimism to increase sales productivity. *Journal of Personal Selling and Sales Management, 19,* 31–37.

Seligman, M. E. P. (1990). *Learned optimism: How to change your mind and your life.* New York: Pocket Books.

Seligman, M. E. P. (1991). *Learned optimism.* New York: Knopf.

Snyder, C. R. (1994). *The psychology of hope: You can get there from here.* New York: Free Press.

Sull, D. N., & Houlder, D. (2005). Do your commitments match your convictions? *Harvard Business Review, 83*(1), 82–91.

Sutcliffe, K. M., & Vogus, T. J. (2003). Organizing for resilience. In K. S. Cameron, J. E. Dutton, & R. E. Quinn (Eds.), *Positive organizational scholarship: Foundations of a new discipline* (pp. 94–110). San Francisco: Berrett-Koehler.

Taylor, S. E., & Brown, J. D. (1988). Illusion and well-being: A social psychological perspective on mental health. *Psychological Bulletin, 103,* 193–210.

Thompson, S. (2004). Leading from the eye of the storm. *Educational Leadership, 61*(7), 60–63.

Weick, K. E. (2003). Positive organizing and organizational tragedy. In K. S. Cameron, J. E. Dutton, & R. E. Quinn (Eds.), *Positive organizational scholarship: Foundations of a new discipline* (pp. 66–80). San Francisco: Berrett-Koehler.

Werner, E. E., & Smith, R. S. (1992). *Overcoming the odds: High risk children from birth to adulthood.* Ithaca, NY: Cornell University Press.

Wrzesniewski, A. (2003). Finding positive meaning in work. In K. S. Cameron, J. E. Dutton, & R. E. Quinn (Eds.), *Positive organizational scholarship: Foundations of a new discipline* (pp. 296–308). San Francisco: Berrett-Koehler.

INDEX

About the Authors

Jerry L. Patterson is a professor of leadership studies at the University of Alabama at Birmingham. In his more than 30 years of experience as an educator, he has served as a superintendent, assistant superintendent, elementary school principal, and high school teacher. Patterson has authored seven nationally recognized books, including two published by ASCD, *Productive School Systems for a Nonrational World* (1986) and *Leadership for Tomorrow's Schools* (1993). He has also published more than two dozen articles in professional journals.

Nationally, Patterson has conducted workshops and presentations to more than 20,000 educators and other leaders in 40 states. In addition, he has trained educational leaders in Slovakia, Israel, Nepal, Ecuador, Spain, and Canada. Patterson's focus is in the areas of leadership development, personal and organizational resilience, and culture change.

For information on training, consultation, or other publications, Patterson can be reached at the School of Education, University of Alabama at Birmingham by phone at (205) 975-5946 or e-mail at jpat@uab.edu.

Paul Kelleher serves as the Norine R. Murchison Distinguished Professor and chair of the Department of Education at Trinity University. In his 35-year career in public education, Kelleher served as a superintendent, high school and middle school principal, assistant principal, and teacher.

Kelleher is coauthor, with Tom Sergiovanni, of an educational leadership text. He is also the coauthor of a book on the entry and startup of new school administrators and has written numerous articles.

Kelleher currently serves on the board of directors of the National Society for the Study of Education. He has worked each summer with

Tom Sobol on the staff of the Summer Work Conference for Superintendents at Teachers College, Columbia University.

Kelleher graduated from Harvard College with a BA in English. He
holds an MAT degree from the Harvard Graduate School of Education
and an EdD in educational administration from Teachers' College,
Columbia University.

Kelleher and his wife, Peggy, have a blended family of four grown
children, five grandchildren, and a very special cat, Spunky.

Related ASCD Resources

At the time of publication, the following ASCD resources were available; for the most up-to-date information about ASCD resources, go to www.ascd.org. ASCD stock numbers are noted in parentheses.

Audio

Bold Leadership: The Rocky Path to Excellence by Pam Robbins and Harvey Alvy (Audiotape #202160)

Developing Mentoring Programs for Professional Excellence by Pam Robbins (Audiotape #203082)

Leading and Building Community in the Swampy Lowlands of No Easy Answers by Robert Bastress, Betty Collins, Gail Covington McBride, and Eric Mills (CD # 504310)

Multimedia

Creating the Capacity for Change by Jody Mason Westbrook and Valarie Spiser-Albert (#702118)

Educational Leadership on CD-ROM, 1992-98 (#598223)

Guide for Instructional Leaders, Guide 1: An ASCD Action Tool by Roland Barth, Bobb Darnell, Laura Lipton, and Bruce Wellman (#702110)

Books

The Art of School Leadership by Thomas R. Hoerr (#105037)

From Standards to Success: A Guide for School Leaders by Mark O'Shea (#105017)

The Hero's Journey: How Educators Can Transform Schools and Improve Learning by John L. Brown and Cerylle A. Moffett (#199002)

Lessons from Exceptional School Leaders by Mark F. Goldberg (#101229)

School Leadership That Works: From Research to Results by Robert J. Marzano, Timothy Waters, and Brian A. McNulty (#105125)

Staying Centered: Curriculum Leadership In a Turbulent Era by Steven Jay Gross (#198008)

Networks

Visit the ASCD Web site (www.ascd.org) and search for "networks" for information about professional educators who have formed groups in the categories of "Restructuring Schools" and "Performance Assessment for Leadership." Look in the "Network Directory" for current facilitators' addresses and phone numbers.

For more information, visit us on the World Wide Web (http://www.ascd.org), send an e-mail message to member@ascd.org, call the ASCD Service Center (1-800-933-ASCD or 703-578-9600, then press 2), send a fax to 703-575-5400, or write to Information Services, ASCD, 1703 N. Beauregard St., Alexandria, VA 22311-1714 USA.